Praise for
A ROAD MAP
to Joy

You're not often given the chance to write an endorsement for one of your heroes. Bonnie Saul Wilks is one of mine. *A Road Map to Joy* is not just a book. It is page after page filled with words carefully constructed from the experiences of a life lived in passionate commitment to the God who is the giver of all joy.

Few people have the unique life experience of following our great King on adventure after adventure like Bonnie—and not just following Him begrudgingly but leaning in to the often difficult places He leads us into. Through her masterful grasp of language, Bonnie imparts unique wisdom that can be learned only through trials, victories, and a life lived with steadfast faith.

My wife, Tabatha, and I have been recipients of Bonnie's sage wisdom at critical moments in our lives. Bonnie's book will provide the same experience for each reader.

—NIC LESMEISTER
EXECUTIVE PASTOR, GATEWAY CHURCH

Bonnie is one of those rare voices whose writing flows from a life deeply lived with God. I've had the privilege of watching Bonnie as a friend over the years, and what she carries in person, she pours out on the page—honesty, beauty, and deep spiritual strength. In *A Road Map to Joy*, she gives language to the quiet, often unspoken emotions we all feel but struggle to express. Her words don't just inspire; they restore. This book is a tender, powerful invitation to find beauty in brokenness and joy in the midst of sorrow.

—MICHAEL MISTRETTA
CEO, FELLOWSHIP OF ISRAEL RELATED MINISTRIES

Some people are given a gift to see more and also have the gift of conveying, in splendid writing, the glory of God in life and His good creation. This is even glory in the midst of suffering. Bonnie Saul Wilks is given this gift—a gift that opens us to a divine perspective. "In your light we see light," David the psalmist wrote. Enjoy Bonnie's writing as she opens a window to show us that there is more than the ordinary gaze that one sees. Whether she writes about the shores of Scotland or the experiences of her life history, Bonnie is given the ability from God to touch our hearts.

—DANIEL JUSTER
FOUNDER AND DIRECTOR, TIKKUN
INTERNATIONAL, A NETWORK OF
MINISTRIES FOCUSED ON THE RESTORATION
OF ISRAEL AND THE CHURCH

A Road Map to Joy came to me during the Israeli war. As I read, the weight of disappointment, stress, and discouragement began to lift. As an Israeli citizen, often running for shelter, I hadn't stopped to process the loss and pain within, but Bonnie's book guided me to a fresh perspective during the hardest season of my life. Overflowing with timeless wisdom and fresh, revelatory insight, Bonnie's words wrap around you like a warm embrace, offering comfort, courage, and renewed hope for life's journey. Each story she shares, along with the many sacrifices she has made, reveals more of God's goodness. Every poem reverberates with life, pointing the reader toward the heart of God. Her writing awakens something deep within the soul, connecting and inspiring, comforting and healing from beginning to end, drawing you ever closer to the Lord. I wholeheartedly recommend this book to readers of all ages and walks of life.

—ELISA LEVINE
COFOUNDER, HATIKVA PROJECT

Joy is simple in experience, but finding it can be complex. In a world full of distractions and obstacles, Bonnie provides a road map to joy! She offers fifty clear and practical paths to lasting joy. With wisdom rooted in Scripture and lived experience, this book helps us discover the kind of joy that anchors the soul in every season.

—ELIAS REYES
FOUNDER AND PRESIDENT, MODERN DAY MISSIONS

I cried through these pages. They soothed heartaches, kindled flames of ministry, and prompted arms up from my sides in worship. Ponder. Pray. Act. Let these words work in you. Come, blink your eyes in the bright light of Christ's testimony through Bonnie's life and verse.

—JEN WEAVER
BIBLE TEACHER AND MULTIPUBLISHED
AUTHOR, *A BECKONING TO WONDER: CHRISTIAN POETRY EXPLORING GOD'S STORY*

Bonnie's road map to joy is a great asset for those who are seeking to find and grow joy in troublesome times. She quotes over thirty psalms in this reflective meditation. Reading this book, I am reminded of another—Psalm 34:8 says, "Taste and see that the LORD is good." David certainly modeled this ability in his psalms, and Bonnie empowers the reader to follow suit. This book is a wonderful, meditative read!

—GREG STONE
FOUNDER AND SENIOR PASTOR,
MESSIAH'S HOPE CONGREGATION

You hold in your hand a rare thing. This book is both a dramatic story and a work of art filled with exquisite beauty—I could not put it down. More than that, if you open these pages, you will find yourself on a daily path to deep healing. This is one of the most practical guides to contentment and joy that I have ever read. Thank you, Bonnie.

—JOHN DAWSON
PRESIDENT EMERITUS, YOUTH WITH A MISSION

POEMS AND STORIES

A Road Map to Joy

FIND YOUR WAY IN A WORLD OF DISCONTENT

BONNIE SAUL WILKS

Harp & Sword
MEDIA

A Road Map to Joy by Bonnie Saul Wilks

Published by Harp & Sword Media LLC
129 S. Main St., #260
Grapevine, TX 76051
www.harpandswordmedia.com

Copyright © 2026 by Bonnie Saul Wilks. All rights reserved.

No part of this publication may be reproduced, stored in a retrieval system, or transmitted in any form or by any means—electronic, mechanical, photocopy, recording, or otherwise—except for brief quotations in printed reviews, without the prior written permission of the publisher.

Unless otherwise noted, all Scripture quotations are taken from the Holy Bible, New International Version®, NIV®. Copyright © 1973, 1978, 1984, 2011 by Biblica, Inc.® Used by permission of Zondervan. All rights reserved worldwide. www.zondervan.com. The "NIV" and "New International Version" are trademarks registered in the United States Patent and Trademark Office by Biblica, Inc.®

Scripture quotations marked ESV are from The ESV® Bible (The Holy Bible, English Standard Version®), copyright © 2001 by Crossway, a publishing ministry of Good News Publishers. Used by permission. All rights reserved.

Scripture quotations marked KJV are from the King James Version of the Bible.

Scripture quotations marked NASB are taken from the (NASB®) New American Standard Bible®, Copyright © 1960, 1971, 1977, 1995 by The Lockman Foundation. Used by permission. All rights reserved. www.lockman.org

Scripture quotations marked NET are from the NET Bible® copyright ©1996-2017 by Biblical Studies Press, L.L.C. http://netbible.com. All rights reserved.

Scripture quotations marked NKJV are taken from the New King James Version®. Copyright © 1982 by Thomas Nelson. Used by permission. All rights reserved.

Scripture quotations marked NLT are taken from the Holy Bible, New Living Translation, copyright ©1996, 2004, 2015 by Tyndale House Foundation. Used by permission of Tyndale House Publishers, Carol Stream, Illinois 60188. All rights reserved.

Scripture quotations marked TPT are from The Passion Translation®. Copyright © 2017, 2018, 2020 by Passion & Fire Ministries, Inc. Used by permission. All rights reserved. ThePassionTranslation.com.

Cover and interior design by YOUNG DESIGN, LLC | youngdesignportfolio.com

ISBN (hardcover): 979-8-9997394-5-2
ISBN (hardcover with dust jacket): 979-8-9988032-5-3
ISBN (ebook): 979-8-9988032-6-0

11 10 9 8 7 6 5 4 3 2

Printed in the United States

To Wayne, forever beloved.

…fixing our eyes on Jesus, the pioneer and perfecter of faith. For the joy set before him he endured the cross, scorning its shame, and sat down at the right hand of the throne of God.

—Hebrews 12:2

I sometimes wonder whether all pleasures are not substitutes for joy.

—C. S. Lewis

TABLE OF CONTENTS

THE LIGHT OF JOY XV

INTRODUCTION XVII

NOTE TO THE READER XXI

JOY XXV

1. JOY'S DILEMMA 1

2. BROKENNESS, THE DOOR OF HOPE 7

3. INEFFABLE 15

4. THE SACRIFICIAL SPARK 21

5. KNEELING 29

6. DAZZLING TATTOO 35

7. HEALING 43

8. TABLE OF FORGIVENESS 49

9. QUIET MORNING 55

10. ONE NOD	63
11. GOLD GLUE	69
12. RUSTED FILIGREES	75
13. DESERT PURPLE	81
14. AT THE NAIL SALON	87
15. LAVENDER SHIRT NOT REQUIRED	93
16. THE PANDEMIC	99
17. CONFESSIONS OF A DESPERATE HEART	105
18. THE RIVERBANKS OF TOMORROW	113
19. UPON THIS TREE	119
20. PLEASE PASS THE BREAD	125
21. SHADES OF VIOLET	131
22. UNDERSCORING JUSTICE	137
23. ON AN IRISH CLIFF	145
24. CONFESSIONS OF A COSMIC OUTCAST	151
25. LEANING ON THE STARS	157
26. STABILITY IN NEW BEGINNINGS	161
27. SOUL AND SPIRIT	167

28. KNOWING GOD'S GOODNESS	173
29. FIRST RAIN	179
30. SHE HOPED	185
31. WHERE FLOWERS CRACK THE STONE	193
32. WANT TO EVEN THE SCORE?	199
33. JUSTICE	209
34. THE WHAT, WHEN, AND HOW OF OBEDIENCE	215
35. THE FRAYED HEM	221
36. YOU INTENDED TO HARM ME	227
37. CLOCKS IN ARGENTINA	233
38. SABBATH AS A BRIDE	239
39. TO HOPE	247
40. DEATH BY LOW SALT	253
41. DARK AND SWEET	259
42. CULTURE VERSUS CONTENT	265
43. THE FLOOD	273
44. THE RIGHT TO SPEAK	279
45. YOU SOBERED YOUR SOUL	285

46. TWO STORIES BECOMING ONE	291
47. SKULL HILL	299
48. THE PINK BOMB SHELTER	305
49. TO BEGIN AGAIN	313
50. ANGELS, THE BURNING ONES	319
THE LIGHT OF JOY	331
JOY	333
ENDNOTES	335
ABOUT THE AUTHOR	339

THE LIGHT OF JOY

Happiness is joy's
counterfeit and sorrow
its truest test. When

you finally perceive,
down deep, the price
and prize of redemption,

you are free to bend
life's bruises and victories
into the shape of over-

coming, everlasting joy.
Verbal, sacrificial praise
releases a fountain gate to

an ocean of exuberance
available to those that
bound beyond the

limitations of simple
gratefulness, that have
plunged into the amnesiac

depths of cleansing blood
and just can't stop saying,
thank You, thank You,
thank You!

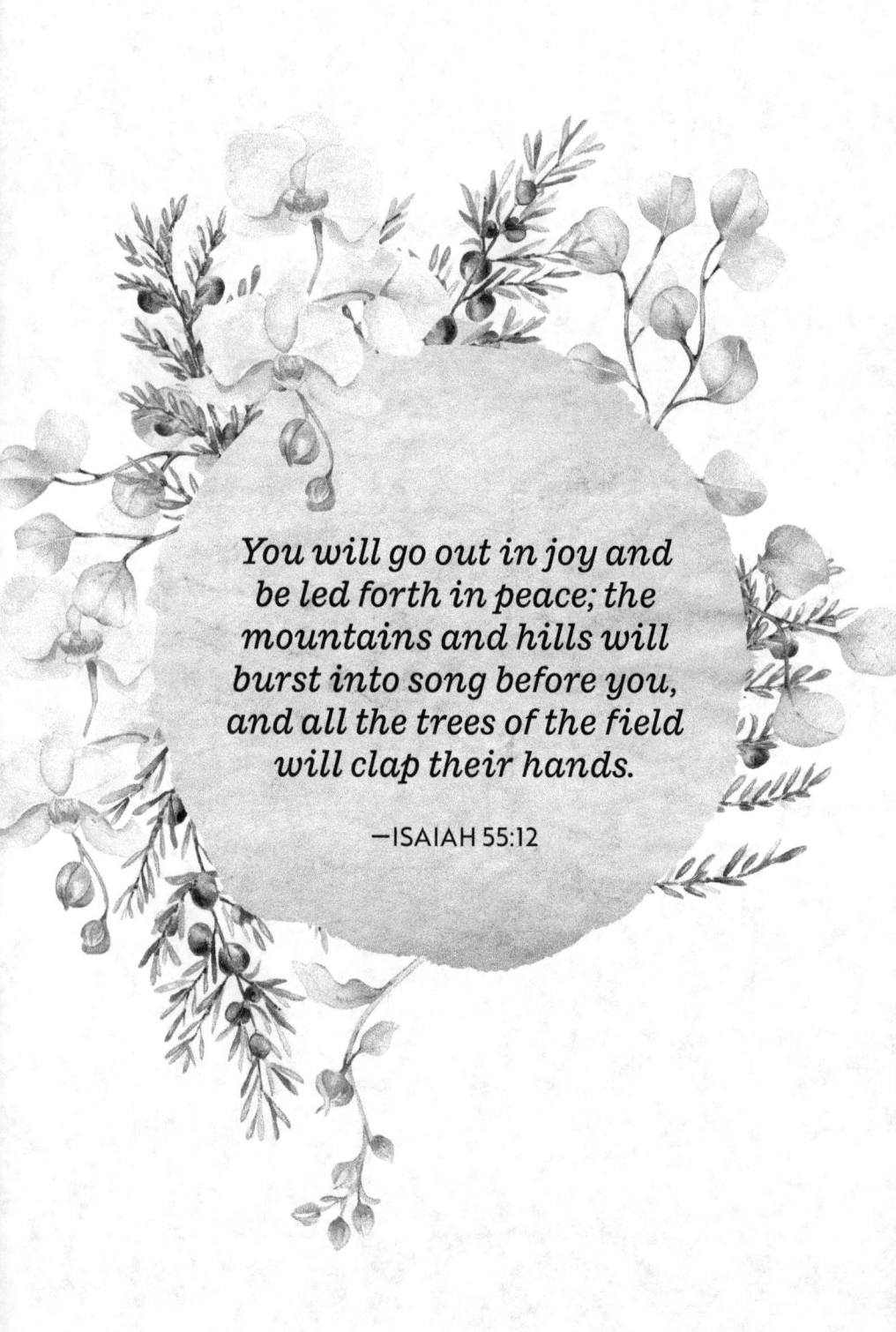

You will go out in joy and be led forth in peace; the mountains and hills will burst into song before you, and all the trees of the field will clap their hands.

—ISAIAH 55:12

Introduction

At 4:30 in the autumn darkness of early morning on November 14, Wayne, our beloved son-in-love, our daughter, and I stepped out of the car and into the brightly lit lobby of the University of Texas Southwestern Medical Center in Dallas, Texas. I admit that morning, we did not leave the house going out in joy.

The surgeons had scheduled my precious husband for prostate cancer surgery at 7 a.m. that day. The hard, cold truth was that I left the warmth and protection of our home in frustration, heaviness, anxiety, a bit of fear—and a little mad at God.

Still, God remained firm and faithful in our uncertainty. He met us. Our everlasting Father offered us joy—not happiness or a glimpse of the ending. Unless you have known supernatural, deep-down joy despite circumstance, you may not believe it exists.

Lifetime friends circled up around Julia, Daniel, and me at the hospital, made us laugh, and reminded us of God's healing power and faithfulness. They sat with us during hours of surgery and hand-wringing waiting. Later, dozens brought food, cards, and gift cards for recovery.

Embracing joy stood within reach that morning, but I couldn't grasp it. Now when I contemplate the situation, I know there is always a reason to offer a sacrifice of praise. Goodness and loving-kindness can always be found in the most unusual and bitter places.

In contrast, when we left the hospital a day later, we did go out in joy—the surgery was a success, and the weight we'd been carrying had lifted. For the moment, the doctors proclaimed a clean bill of health! This news became the best first-day-post-surgery declaration. Yay, God, and hats off to an amazing medical team at Southwestern!

Still, the pathway to joy is an arduous journey. Nothing was certain, even after the doctor's positive report. There would be diet changes, semiannual cancer checkups, and no guarantees of perfect health hereafter. The only promise is that God is always with us and tenderly cares for us in every circumstance. This thought alone ushers in joy!

Joy is available every day and every time we leave home. A believer's journey toward heaven should be characterized by joy. Isaiah 55 illuminates how life's pathway can become an adventure of jubilation.

True joy is God's lavish gift to humankind through the salvation offered by Jesus Christ, freely given to anyone who repents of sins and asks for forgiveness. Joy flows from walking the humble road and holding close to God's ways—which are higher than our own. These actions empower us to develop meekness. By choosing to apply God's life instructions given in His Word, we can experience redemption and fullness of joy.

Scripture gives us the sweet promise that a relationship with Jesus brings "inexpressible and glorious joy" (1 Pet. 1:8). For us as disciples of Christ, joy is the mountain-high part of our journey that helps us through the low valleys. The Christian life is a journey of following Jesus, the only way to heaven. Every step is led by the Holy Spirit, who guides us into truth and transformation. Though joy and sorrow often run on parallel tracks, we are sustained by the living water Christ offers—an eternal gift that satisfies our deepest need. With each dip into the depths of God's Word, we can find renewed joy.

Take hold of joy during heartache. Choose joy. Go out in joy. He will meet you with concrete, life-sustaining strength, and you will find a reason to go out with joy.

C. S. Lewis, one of the most significant Christian writers of our time, has delved into the meaning of supernatural joy more than any modern writer, expressing and defining its essence and foundation. His insights have profoundly influenced my faith journey. For me, Lewis' pathway toward God became a road map of how to find beauty in all circumstances. His example of choosing joy in the face of death has gripped my heart. Truly he is a master storyteller. The Chronicles of Narnia will remain a favorite of mine forever! Lewis' descriptions of beauty and joy, found first in God and echoed in humanity and the universe, are penetrating, weighty, and enlightened. My heart races when I read words like these from Lewis on beauty and joy:

> You might as well offer a mutton chop to a man who is dying of thirst as offer of sexual pleasure to the desire.... Joy is not a substitute for sex; sex is very often a substitute for Joy. I sometimes wonder whether all pleasures are not substitutes for Joy.[1]

In current American culture, and indeed the entire world, there rages a relentless drive within each heart for the fleeting pursuit of pleasure. In many of Lewis' books he beautifully explains how humankind is created with a longing for something beyond oneself. Perhaps this looks like romanticism or nostalgia. Perhaps a sweet memory or a roaring river sparks this deep yearning. We fill this hole with so many material things. Indeed, the only relief and fulfillment of this hope for more is the joy we find in union with Christ. God alone created our inner yearning, and we should not ignore it. We must seriously embrace that the pleasures of the world vastly fail in bringing deep fulfillment to the hungry. Once this issue is settled in our hearts, the door opens, and the true joy of Jesus fills the human body, soul, and spirit to the brim overflowing.

My husband, Wayne, and daughter, Julia, packed our belongings in 1996 to live in Odesa, Ukraine. The flames of Communism had just gone underground, and Soviet people longed for the truth of the gospel. Evangelistic teams rushed in, and there began a rival and a renewal of Christianity in the former Soviet Union.

From there we traveled the world for twenty-two years. I began to keep a diary of our experiences and my dealings with the Lord along our journey. Most of these musings were written in poetry, some in devotional thoughts, and a few in essays. The daily routine of rigorous travel and living out of suitcases sometimes became heavy. Somewhere in my frail obedience God met me. I learned to be grateful and to express thanksgiving. I learned to find beauty and make a cozy home in every place. I wrote about it often and have kept a blog since 2007 (bonniewilks.com).

On the following pages we will discover pathways to joy together through the lens of my personal life experiences as a woman of faith, a wife, a mother, a missionary, and a poet. I'm eager to share my journey with you in fifty pathways to joy.

Note to the Reader

I love words. With certain ones I see color in shimmering sheets or taste things like cinnamon or cheese. For instance, the word *scarlet* is a sparkling expanse of the color. With the word *indent*, I taste and feel chewing gum. Weird, right? I considered this normal and never told anyone until late in life. Then, my dear friend Emma explained to me this phenomenon called synesthesia, which means dual senses in Greek. It is the sensory ability to taste or see color with some words or numbers or to see or taste a sound. Only about 2–4 percent of the population has synesthesia. It's like color blindness in reverse. The sad thing is that it dims with age.

Synesthesia does not enhance my writing or anything. Bummer. Still, the love of words drew me to the dictionary at a young age. I relished reading it and learning. My mother-in-law owned a larger-than-life dictionary, which found its home on an intricately carved wooden pedestal. How appropriate, I thought, as I approached looking up words as an almost holy act.

As a student I did not enjoy poetry—it didn't seem worth the time required to uncover its meaning. Rhyming appeared trite. Then, a very strange thing happened in my high school English class when the instructor assigned each student the task of composing a poem. She warned us against plagiarizing, emphasizing that she would immediately recognize it! We had only a week to finish the assignment. Never being motivated academically, I put little effort into my studies, which labeled me "average" in some subjects, such as math. The challenge of composing original verses scared me, so I scribbled a few mediocre, non-rhyming lines and called it finished.

When my best friend discovered how quickly I had completed the assignment, she asked if I would write her poem. I agreed because—honestly, I don't know why I did it! Serendipitously, the challenge released an uncultivated writing gift and interest in poetry. It moved me beyond laziness, the fruit of it, and the limited academic output previously confining me. Suddenly, under a pseudonym, I had been granted the gift and pleasure of writing something the teacher did not recognize as mine. I soared at the opportunity, and now I wish the poem could be found—my friend won an award for it. The verses were published in a high school anthology of poetry for our state. My friend begged me to keep this secret, which I did until now. Wow, the memory boggles my mind to this day.

Years later, after marriage, I remembered my brush with fame and incognito poetry and decided to start reading and studying poetry in earnest. My husband was a PhD student at the University of Texas in Denton and had access to a fabulous library. Weekly he brought me scores of poetry books and critical analyses of poetry. I delightfully and voraciously enveloped them and soon after began writing my own verses. I discovered release, purpose, and most of all, precision in expression. Writing poetry became the best form of catharsis for frustration and trauma, and effective resistance against the things in life I could not change. Words and verses became a tool of survival. Streams of joy flooded my heart when I wrote.

When my husband, my daughter, and I were released into the mission field during my midlife, writing became a lifeline and a lifeboat. It stood as my black-and-white documentation of experiences and way to grapple with conflicting feelings through so much change. On our first trip to Russia, the poems poured out with every new experience—people, food, language, culture, history, beauty, and the fall of Communism. That group of poems stands today as the legacy for an important period in our lives.

This practice has continued to bring clarity and hope into my life, and most importantly, in this context—*joy*. I have included twenty-five poems or prose poems in this book, as well as twenty-five essays. With each poem, I have done something that poets rarely do—include an explanation of why the poem was written, where I was, and what I thought. This is not to deter the reader from drawing their own conclusions or thoughts while reading but to stand as a springboard for personal inspiration.

At the end of each chapter you will find scriptures, prayers, activations, and book recommendations as we navigate the road map to joy. Each entry stands uniquely on its own. I pray this handbook becomes a compass and a guide as you find your way to joy.

—Bonnie

JOY

Joy is something you swallow in big, lavish gulps, and something you exude—to give away—like perfumed ointment.

> No soul that seriously and constantly desires joy will ever miss it. Those who seek find. To those who knock it is opened.
>
> —C. S. LEWIS

Joy's Dilemma

My treasured keepsakes bulge in pockets of time—or rather moments—tucked hard against the bones of my heart. They remain as fresh and life-giving as the first offerings of spring rosebuds, tight with fragrance and bleeding crimson, which smears across my fingers as I pull out one petal at a time. The edges are velvety but frayed—somehow old and young at once.

As both a child and adult, I've sat at the piano with Bach or Chopin for two or three hours at a time, in awe of such a remote and deep connection. I've lived close to the blue Danube and sprinkled my food with the richest *paprikash* of Hungarian delight. The deep, foreboding underground metro in Moscow scarred and scared me awake, as did Lenin's black marble tomb. The silver chopsticks of Korea dubbed me an amateur on the hard floor of a church basement. My muscles revolted in pain, but the days of kindred fellowship rose higher than the inconvenience.

I've enfolded prayers into the cracks of the Western Wall and witnessed the great religions of the world collapse into obscurity at Skull Hill's empty sepulchre.

I've allowed the Psalms of Ethiopia to wash over me in Addis Ababa as tears flowed for the marrow of civilization in the light of eternity. The elegant Ethiopians walked across my belly and touched the palms of my hands, and the beat of their prayer sticks lifted my soul and feet to praise. To this day part of me has never really left that country.

I've admired the ancient terracing of Cyprus just before sundown when shadows lengthen in beauty, and I've drooled over the tender buds of almond flowers breaking open, wild with hope.

The faded Kodak photograph of two-year-old Bonnie sitting on my grandpa Saul's lap lives on as if it happened yesterday, as do the promises and kisses of marriage at the altar in a flurry of ivory, lace, and the palest lavender.

Years later my husband and I lived from suitcase to airplane, stood on three continents in one week, and proclaimed that the one true God is the exact image of Jesus.

We knew more of weakness than strength
and asked for grace to fear the Lord,
where all obedience begins and ends.

Now I hug my grandbabies and realize my pockets holding moments are full and deep. I'll keep jamming the seasons into the ample, unbuttoned openings until the seams bust—bust with joy—

Joy for more,
And the ultimate joy of no more.

ROAD MAP TO JOY

At age forty I began to feel on the verge of a midlife crisis. As my unhappiness grew, I began to pray. The Lord responded with a simple and piercing message in my heart, "You're ungrateful." Oh, I was thankful and could recognize a job well done or a thoughtful gesture, but I had never developed a lifestyle of gratitude, which is something completely different. Immediately I worked on my attitude toward my surroundings and began expressing heartfelt words of grace, praise, and gratitude about everything, good or bad. This muscle hurt when I first started stretching it in earnest. Now it has grown into a coursing river of joy in my life that has taken me to the heights of beautiful mountains and depths of valleys overcome through praise.

Scripture
"You make known to me the path of life; you will fill me with joy in your presence, with eternal pleasures at your right hand" (Ps. 16:11).

Prayer
Dear Lord, I thank You for showing me the path of life, sometimes just a day at a time. Each sunrise offers blessings and hardships. Please help me trust You in hard times, choose

thanksgiving, and pray earnestly about all things. Thank You for giving me joy in abundance when I ask for it.

Activation
If your life needs a boost of joy, begin living a life of gratitude by becoming more aware of your blessings, being grateful for your hardships, and verbally expressing your appreciation for those around you. Take concrete steps to thank, recognize, and honor those who have contributed to your successes and achievements.

Further Study
Acts 2:28, Jude 1:24, and Psalm 36:7–8

Recommended Reading
Choose Joy Women's Devotional: Finding Joy No Matter What You're Going Through by Kay Warren, and *Surprised by Joy: The Shape of My Early Life* by C. S. Lewis

Deep hides the green leaf buried in the twisted bramble of winter branch.

2

Brokenness, the Door of Hope

Hardship often prepares an ordinary person for an extraordinary destiny.
—*The Chronicles of Narnia: The Voyage of the Dawn Treader*

Undoubtedly the hardest years of my life were in Ukraine when we first moved there. After the fall of Communism, some cities and villages remained nearly a century behind the United States, making it difficult for spoiled, pampered Americans to survive. Everything in my life had turned upside down, and there seemed no comfort or recourse but to endure. I hated it. I griped for one solid year, until I broke and finally surrendered in joy to God's will for my life. It came after many tears, anger, and fighting against it. There was nothing to take pleasure in but God. It sounds terrible, but it's true. God brought me there to show me how fulfilling He alone is.

God was seeking my steady affection and trust through the storm.

The first Messianic Jewish Bible Institute began in a small fishing village, Myaki, about fifty kilometers outside of Odesa, Ukraine, in an old Communist indoctrination camp for Russian youth. Located at the end of an unpaved road lined with homes made with mud bricks and thatched roofs, the village resembled something out of *Fiddler on the Roof*.

Sometimes the wind blew so hard through the windows that it would blow the candles out on the table. Our first winter in Ukraine was one of the coldest they had had in twenty-five years. We often went without heat, electricity, and water. It was a rough beginning. I wanted to return to my warm home in Texas nearly every day for the first year.

One morning stands out vividly in my memory. The heat and electricity were out once again, so Julia and I were in the kitchen, bundled up in our winter coats, hats, scarves, and mittens. The room was frigid. Julia worked on her homeschooling for the day, while I endeavored to cook an egg for her breakfast. Suddenly the stove stopped working too. I just looked at that raw egg staring me in the face.

I told Julia she couldn't have an egg for breakfast, and she suddenly stood up and burst into tears. Julia was only eight years old at the time and had been very courageous through all the rough transitions that life in Ukraine demanded of her. I wasn't surprised to see such an emotional outburst.

She finally caught her breath, and between sobs she said, "Mama, Mama, I feel like I am losing my life."

I ran to her, throwing my arms around her neck. I sobbed too. After a couple of minutes I said, "Julia, I feel like I am losing my life too. In fact, we are both losing our lives. Jesus granted us the privilege of losing our lives. Something dies in us so that something can live in others."

Though it was a hard moment, I would not trade for all the memories of Julia's childhood. It was a lesson lived in living color about embracing the irony of God's kingdom—about how you really find your life when you lose it.

We stayed in Myaki for our first MJBI school year. Now I recall it as the sweetest year of my life. God's grace lifted us through those times and carried our family through the rough times. It was a year full of contradictions—the stark difference between the warm fuzzies you feel at the church altar when responding to an emotional call to the mission field and the cold reality of living it out in a foreign place. There were extreme highs and lows while trying to stay true to what God had called us to do through a torrent of emotions.

I would have given up and gone home, but somehow God allowed me to stay. I would have turned back and said, "Forget it. It is too hard." But God just wouldn't let me do that, because He wanted all the credit for the humble beginning of the school.

I know He deserves the credit because I quit every day for one year.

Many mornings I wouldn't want to get out of bed, but I would hear the first students praying and singing out to God, asking Him to reveal Himself to the Jewish people of Ukraine. Though accustomed to rough situations, the students knew we were suffering, and I know they prayed for us too. Those prayers sustained us.

It is hard to believe several decades have passed. God has done amazing things over the past few years. I believe the best is yet to be.

When I count my blessings, I consider myself favored by God, as He allowed such suffering in my life to strengthen my faith and enable me to serve Him more purely and trust Him more fully. In the end the blessings in my life have overtaken the little that I suffered!

Time and experience have proved that the setbacks, disappointments, suffering, and betrayals of my life have turned out for good. Truly they have become a door of hope—opening to wonderful opportunities of the heart and circumstance—to love the Lord and the body of Messiah more purely and fully. Although never comfortable to endure, the affliction of my soul or body has led me right to the arms of Jesus, who has showered me with comfort, love, and a pathway of escape.

ROAD MAP TO JOY

Job 36:15 (NET) says, "He delivers the afflicted by [way of] their afflictions." I love this verse! When we are in the middle of pain and there seems no recourse but to endure, we seek an immediate solution to escape from the suffering or problem. But it is written here that God makes a path to relief by way of the affliction. It means you must hold steady and look to God for comfort and guidance amid the pain. In time He will faithfully bring you to resolve and a peaceful place of respite. In fact, during the conflict there is shelter in prayer and covering as you seek His face rather than the answer to the conflict.

God doesn't call everyone to live abroad in an underdeveloped nation, but He does call each to pick up their cross and follow Him. God calls all of us to share the good news with the world, starting at home.

Scripture
"For this light momentary affliction is preparing for us an eternal weight of glory beyond all comparison, as we look not to the things that are seen but to the things that are unseen" (2 Cor. 4:17–18, ESV).

Prayer
Dear Lord, I accept that following You and sharing my testimony with others is costly. Remind me of the price You paid for me. Give me the grace, strength, and joy to persevere when I feel overwhelmed by the trials of life.

Activation
Identify a burden in your life that requires you to give up your own will for the betterment of a person or situation. Ask God for opportunities to share the gospel. The Good Shepherd will strengthen your resolve to press on in joy.

Further Study
Job 36:10, 2 Chronicles 12:8, and Romans 5:3–4

Recommended Reading
Suffering Is Never for Nothing by Elisabeth Elliot, and *He Chose the Nails: What God Did to Win Your Heart* by Max Lucado

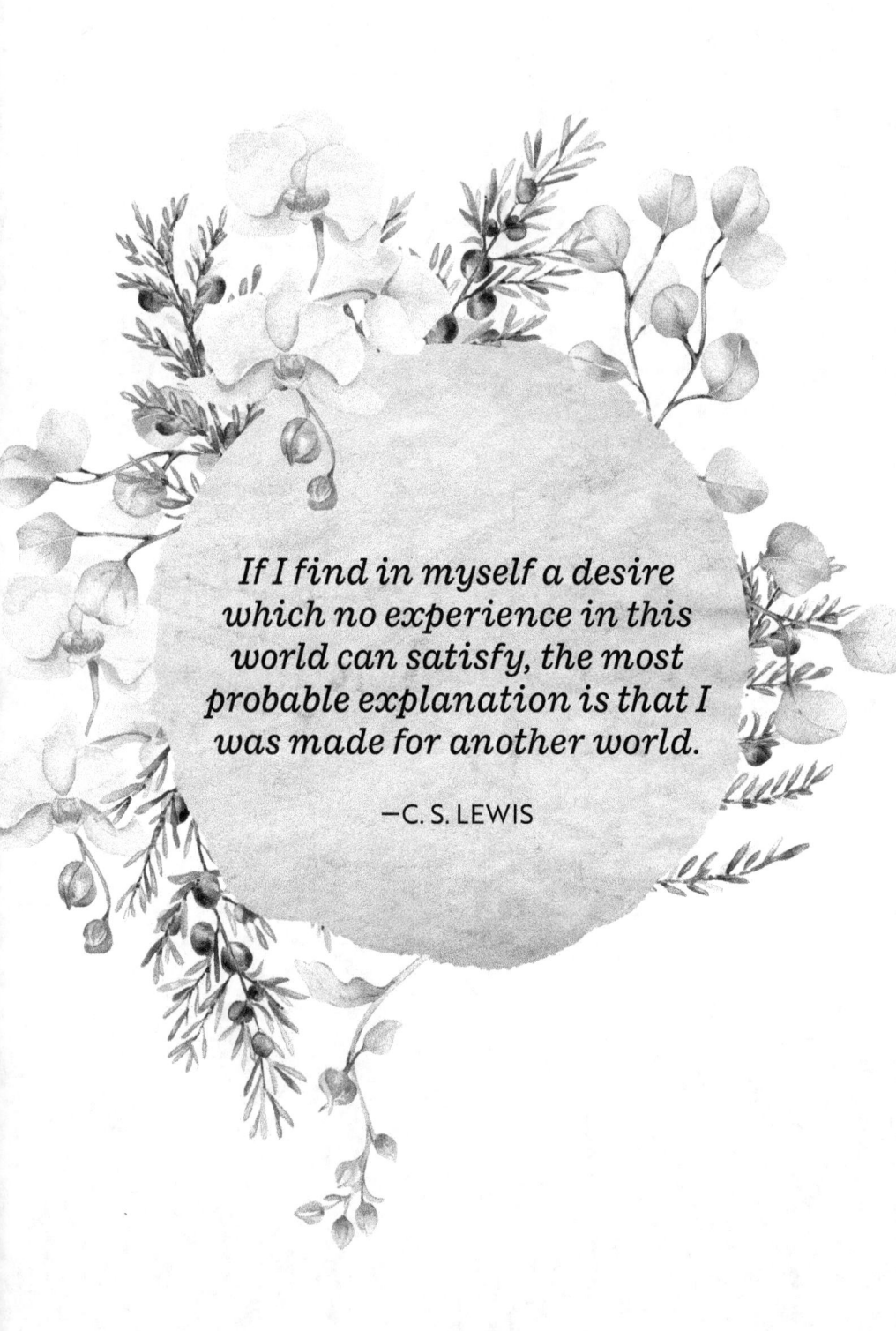

If I find in myself a desire which no experience in this world can satisfy, the most probable explanation is that I was made for another world.

—C. S. LEWIS

3

Ineffable

Remember when we watched—mesmerized by the majestic deer on distant highlands, feeding at noon? And our friends exclaimed, "How intriguing for this time of day!" The ground shook. Sun, moon, and stars broke to pause

and peer for a lifetime of five seconds. It was the cry of the seagulls and arcs of their wings connecting heaven and earth that sealed our captivity upon the mossy-grown craggy cliffs of the Scottish northern shores. It took our

breath away—and thought we might die for beauty. Fall we did, as trees are felled. On our faces, we wept with the skies—lavish silvery

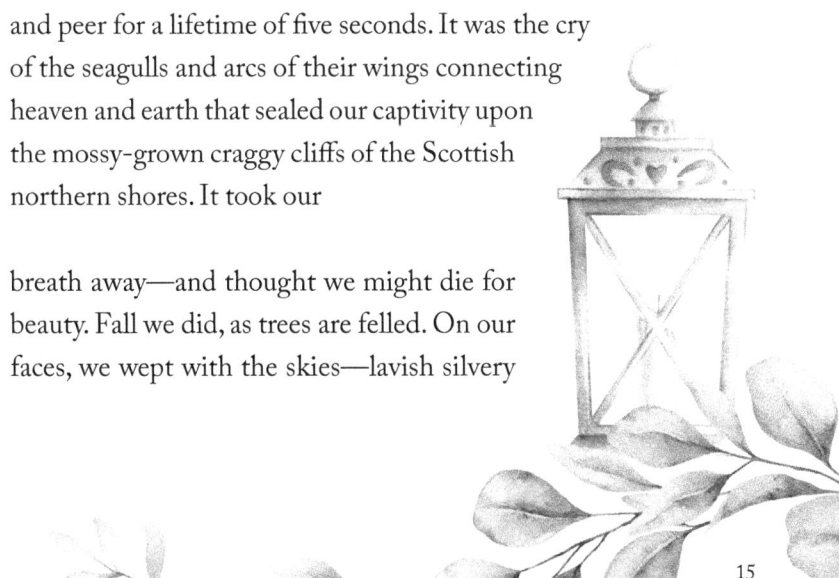

tears of rain—for life and death and the longing to go home.
We lingered for more and all the

more, then rose and praised our kind Maker. To be held prisoner of this exquisiteness is a privilege, for it piques and pales in comeliness and value compared to the savage beauty of blood and water, bruises, stripes,

piercings, and injustice for justice. We blinked our eyes again and again for holiness and purity and untouchable, blinding light. Walking from the mountaintop to the northern shores, like Miriam, we raised our

tambourines to the music beat of a divine score. There is no God like Yahweh! There is no God like Yah! We measured the distance between heaven and earth and the depth of the North Sea and counted a thousand

Scottish bluebells nestled between the heather—each blossom tinged with scarlet drops of love. All the way down the mountain, we flew dancing and singing and speaking ineffable mysteries.

—*Written at Blairmore House, Huntly, Scotland*

ROAD MAP TO JOY

I'm grateful for the opportunity to travel extensively internationally. Often I am asked what my favorite country is, but it's hard to choose from the abundance of beauty around the world. Currently my absolute favorite is Scotland. We were blessed to be there for nearly two weeks, and I became enthralled with the vast and scarry awesomeness of the coastland, mountains, and moors. Some places on the northern shores are remote from man, yet I sensed a nearness to God. I felt small compared with the splendor before me, yet I knew that God had noticed me and that my life and thoughts mattered to Him. The beauty became nourishing and profound, and it became easy to imagine that God's love toward me was as extravagant as the comeliness of the creation before me. I found several "thin places" there where the veil between heaven and earth became transparent or gossamer, where the goodness of God unfolded as an offer of friendship, tangible and compelling. In these holy spaces I understood that a face-to-face, meaningful relationship with Him was possible. This brush with the weighty presence of the heavenly realm changed me forever and brought immeasurable joy!

Scripture

"There are three things that are too amazing for me, four that I do not understand: the way of an eagle in the sky, the way of a snake on a rock, the way of a ship on the high seas, and the way of a man with a young woman" (Prov. 30:18–19).

Prayer

I thank You, Lord, for creating the universe for our delight. I know You receive pleasure in our joy over what You have made. I thank You for this glorious world, which my heart can barely contain. Open my eyes to the joys both hidden and seen before me daily.

Activation

Endeavor to get into nature daily and talk to or meditate on God. It is as important and valuable as nourishing yourself with rest and food. Deep joy is found in the beauty of the wellspring of creation—you don't need to travel far from home to derive the benefit of immediate joy.

Further Study
Job 42:3, Psalm 139:6, and Psalm 8:3–4

Recommended Reading
Thin Places: Recognizing When God Breaks Through by Jeff Jernigan, PhD, BCPC, FAIS, and Nancy Jernigan, PhD, LPF LPC; and *Braving the Thin Places: Celtic Wisdom to Create a Space for Grace* by Julianne Stanz

Gratefulness is the tiny sacrificial kindling that sparks the roaring flames of thanksgiving.

4

The Sacrificial Spark

> Gratitude exclaims, very properly, "How good of God to give me this."
> —C. S. Lewis

Recently I felt anxiety while driving to a dental appointment I was dreading. As I began to analyze the feeling, clarity settled. The apprehension originated from a multitude of nagging disappointments and formidable changes, not just the looming dentist's visit.

There were so many sad developments surrounding my life and the people I loved—not to mention our own culture and the world! These shifts were serious, life-altering challenges for the people involved—unexpected or terminal illnesses, deaths, and the trials of daily living. I felt heartsick.

Tears welled in my eyes and ran in rivers down my cheeks. Surprisingly I spontaneously started singing a beloved hymn from my childhood, "Great Is Thy Faithfulness." Anxiety and racing thoughts melted away as I arrived at my appointment. I patted my face dry, drew in a cleansing breath, and released my burden before facing the dentist's drill.

> Here's the deal: God didn't need my praise. I needed to do it as an act of faith and resistance against life's hardships and suffering.

I felt lighter after expressing to the Lord that I know He remains faithful amidst my pain.

Thanking God is a sacrifice at times, but it is an act of honoring Him. Truly, the Lord of all creation doesn't need my thanksgiving, but when I offer it, I grow less self-centered and more assured of His sweet and caring presence in life.

Later, when I was driving home from my office visit, I remembered something from years ago.

When I felt a midlife crisis brewing, I prayed and heard the Lord say, "You're ungrateful." That gentle nudge from the Father shook me awake, so I began slowly developing a lifestyle of gratitude. Like taking bitter medicine, it was difficult at first. Sometimes my words of gratefulness sounded forced, stiff, and cold. I didn't feel gratitude, even though I was trying to express praise to God for all things.

I flat didn't feel it.

But the seed that fell onto the cold, hard ground of my heart grew into a fruit-bearing tree of joyfulness and stability.

Shake off the dark clouds of complacency, anxiety, and fear by expressing thanksgiving to God and to those around you who have contributed to your life and have made you who you are today.

FOUR ADVANTAGES OF GRATITUDE

Redirects Focus

The troubles in life are great and numerous, but God does not want you to bear their weight or focus on them. Redirecting your focus honors Him and puts Him in the right place above the heartache. He is, after all, the Lord of all creation and the Savior of the world. We must see Him during the storm and honor Him for being there.

Reduces Apprehension

Many people in the world live with high anxiety and stress. Eventually this wears your mind, body, and emotions down. It makes it harder to overcome everyday battles. Praising Jesus and declaring Him as the victor in your life reduces apprehension. For many matters in life I just don't have words, so I pray in tongues. The Holy Spirit knows what needs to be said to the Father. When

I am done praying, God has heard, and we have connected. I feel anxiety fall away.

Renews Relationship

Life is about one important thing: a relationship with God through Jesus Christ. Expressing gratitude to Him for who He is and what He has done is always appropriate, especially when we are downcast. This simple act will renew and strengthen our relationship with Him. It will assure us that He is still in control.

Reignites Faith

Expressing gratitude fans the flames of our love for God. He has extravagantly offered us grace and mercy. In return, our hearts should fill with lavish gratitude for all He has done. This simple act will make your love for Him white hot.

Gratefulness is the tiny spark of sacrificial kindling that stokes the roaring flames of thanksgiving and faith, enabling you to overcome.

ROAD MAP TO JOY

Be anxious for nothing, but in everything by prayer and supplication, with thanksgiving, let your requests be made known to God; and the peace of God, which surpasses all understanding, will guard your hearts and minds through Christ Jesus.
—Philippians 4:6–7, NKJV

Every believer grows up with this scripture. At first, it sounds redundant and reused because we have quoted it for so many years. But we need to make our requests known to God with thanksgiving. This is the key element for when we are overwhelmed. Let us pray and petition God for change but always remain thankful.

Scripture
"Rejoice always, pray continually, give thanks in all circumstances; for this is God's will for you in Christ Jesus" (1 Thess. 5:16–18).

Prayer
Dear Lord, sometimes the pressures of life cause me to withdraw my affection and gratitude from You. Please help me trust You and continue to pray for breakthrough and offer thanksgiving.

Activation
Keep a running list of prayers of thanksgiving throughout the seasons of the year. Read them at the year's end. Your heart will flood with gratitude to see how God has been involved in your life on every level.

Further Study
Proverbs 3:5–6, 1 Peter 5:7, and Matthew 6:25–33

Recommended Reading
The Power of Thank You: Discover the Joy of Gratitude by Joyce Meyer, and *Choosing Gratitude: Your Journey to Joy* by Nancy Leigh DeMoss

My feet and journey are flawed as I bear upon the mountains the beauty of a flawless message.

5

Kneeling

Jesus Christ did not say, "Go into all the world and tell the world that it is quite right." The Gospel is something completely different. In fact, it is directly opposed to the world.
—C. S. Lewis

I've spent a lifetime bandaging my feet, partly from ill-fitting shoes, traveling too many miles in a day, losing my way, making a wrong turn, or carrying too many burdens. Also, there are

the roads I've traveled
long just to gaze upon
ancient stones, a rusted
filigree, or become dizzy
with the scent of an
old English rose. My Sender
declares my feet beautiful,
bruised and scarred as
they are. I can hardly
take that in, and only
see it with eyes of faith.

When finishing my course,
I long to be remembered
for bowed knees, for
bowing in indentured
gratefulness, worshipping
my Beloved, calling in
the harvest, falling
upon my face with joy
and tears mingled. Yes,
kneeling. It's what
empowers me to go,
and the best reason
to linger before I go
again.

ROAD MAP TO JOY

As a missionary, I love the scripture "And how can anyone preach unless they are sent? As it is written, 'How beautiful are the feet of those who bring good news'" (Rom. 10:15).

As we traveled from country to country over the years, I cherished every word, especially as I aged and didn't feel the physical stamina of my youth. In fact, my feet felt ugly. The intensity of the journey and the sheer number of miles left them bruised and scarred. While my feet didn't look beautiful, for me the words of Scripture could only be received through faith. Every time I kneeled or paused to worship and linger in the presence of the Lord, I lost myself in His beauty and love. I gained the strength to get up and go again, to share the good news far and wide. Truly, it is in surrender that we have the strength and drive to go into all the world and preach the gospel. Everything happens in prayer.

Scripture
"He said to them, 'Go into all the world and preach the gospel to all creation'" (Mark 16:15).

Prayer
Dear Lord, thank You for the call to go into the world and share the good news. In prayer, this mandate is fulfilled, and You enable me to do the impossible. I thank You for promising to answer my prayers as I kneel and linger.

Activation
Don't be afraid of lingering in prayer. Take time to listen. Lean in to silence and waiting before God. There is great joy and strength in His presence. God will speak to you and give you a divine purpose. If you listen closely, you may find yourself living in a foreign country with tired and bruised but beautiful feet and a heart bursting with joy.

Further Study
Matthew 28:19, Acts 1:8, and Psalm 96:3

Recommended Reading
Let the Nations Be Glad!: The Supremacy of God in Missions by John Piper, and *The Cross and the Switchblade* by David Wilkerson, John Sherrill, and Elizabeth Sherrill

Every day, I allow the beauty of nature to lead me to the cross. There I am undone and captivated. He has pierced my ear with an awl, yet he has not called me slave, but rather daughter of light.

Dazzling Tattoo

"We are told that Christ was killed for us, that His death has washed out our sins, and that by dying He disabled death itself. That is the formula. That is Christianity. That is what has to be believed."
—C. S. Lewis, Mere Christianity

Disgust boiled up in my heart whenever I saw one. The crucifix stung of death, and I loathed it. No matter how small or artistically created, it loomed before me as a grotesque object, representing another man's religion and pathway that may or may not lead heavenward.

My religious upbringing inadvertently taught me to pass over the suffering and death chapters of the "greatest story ever told." Instead, it emphasized the glorious resurrection of Jesus. My perspective changed when my husband and I visited Rome a few years ago.

We had joined an intercessory prayer team that gathered to intercede for reconciliation between Jews and gentiles. Rome was chosen as the setting to highlight the ancient Church's years of cruel treatment toward the Jewish people.

One prayer journey led us to an old Jewish ghetto where God's Chosen People had been isolated from the city. We learned that when outside the ghetto, Romans forced Jews to wear bright yellow clothes for identification. Jewish people were mocked and coerced to participate in parades led by church leaders while onlookers pitched trash at them.

We circled an ancient fountain just outside the ghetto while two devout Catholics led the prayer. Weeping as they expressed heartfelt words, they declared that the precious wounds of Jesus would cover the heinous sins against the Jewish people. At the end they washed the feet of the Messianic Jewish believers who united with us. The prayers and actions of these two believers chipped away at the sharp angles of my heart. I wept too in that ghetto, imagining my own terrible sins, which had caused the wounds of Jesus. For the first time, I gazed ever into the mutilated body of Jesus.

Transformation blossomed in my heart, and a deep appreciation for the cross sprang up. A clarion message rang out to me—the lowest point of Messiah's life was not to be diminished but magnified as the shining pinnacle of His glorious triumph over sin and death.

Some believers may regard the cross with too much zeal, while others may carry deep contempt for it. But there is a middle ground. First Corinthians 1:23–24 (esv) says we are to "preach Christ [Messiah] crucified, a stumbling block to Jews and folly to Gentiles, but to those who are called, both Jews and Greeks, Christ the power and wisdom of God." Because Jesus died on a cross, it is now a precious symbol to me—not to be worshipped but to epitomize my desperate need for blood atonement.

The symbol of the cross deeply encouraged me during one of the most difficult times of my life while living in Myaki, just off the Black Sea. A rustic and cheerless place, we encountered many cultural misunderstandings and physical discomforts. During this time, I remember taking a long walk and spotting a large, rusty, old cross someone had leaned against a building. I snapped a picture of it because it seemed out of place in this archaic village.

I believe God knew its representation would draw me to the only Source of strength. I paused and soaked in its crude form. Corroded and rough with dirt and sharp corners, it had no earthly beauty or value. But its unattractive and feeble appearance bore witness that Jesus had suffered for me, and in turn, I had been given the privilege of suffering, in some small way, for Him.

Lest I forget Thine agony… lead me to Calvary.[2]

How good it is for us to linger and gaze into the depth of Jesus' physical suffering. It should change our lives irrevocably. At Calvary, Jesus' own body changed irrevocably. To this day, Jesus bears the scars that led Him up Golgotha and beyond. Isaiah 49:14–16 recounts Zion's complaint to God that she has been forgotten. In response, the Lord says that even though a mother may forget her nursing child, He will never forget her. The sign of this remembrance is engraved on Jesus' hands. His scars are a flashing neon sign to Israel that He has not forgotten her. Messiah loves her so much that she is cut into His very flesh.

In the Torah, the first five books of the Old Testament, if a slave willingly desired to serve his master for life, his ear was pierced with an awl (Exod. 21:6). The slave no longer needed to be forced to stay, the pierced ear proving his devotion. Jesus' pierced body proves the same. He has not loved or stayed with us by coercion but willingly promised never to leave us. The permanent scarring of His body is proof of His allegiance for eternity.

In the new covenant, Thomas told the disciples that he would not believe in the resurrection unless he saw Jesus' scars. One day Jesus appeared and told Thomas not only to look upon the wounds but to experience them through touch. He said whoever believes without seeing is blessed.

Today we have not seen, but we have experienced the power of His scars. The world may never see a physical sign upon our bodies, but they will know that we follow Jesus by our love for Him and for one another. This unseen tattoo should dazzle like the noonday sun at midnight.

Someday, when the agony of war against the world, sin, and the flesh is over, the bride will join the Bridegroom on the other side. All the earthly seals like piercings will be gone. The symbols of crosses will pass away in paradise, and we will never ponder them again.

But the nail prints. The nail prints will not fade. Our eyes will never tire of gazing into the scarred flesh that bears the form of one He loves so much—Israel. This truth encourages me when I think about things like anti-Semitism, terrorism, natural disasters, war, and the spiritual condition of the world.

At times, both Jews and gentiles shake their fists at God, saying He has forgotten them. Then I remember the nail prints. Those dazzling tattoos engraved into His hands, feet, and side cry out to Israel and the whole world, now and forever, that we are not forgotten.

We have been shown extravagant compassion by extreme measure.

Someday I will place my trembling hand into Jesus' and feel His deep engravings. I know they will burn as a flaming seal forever, for His love is stronger than death.

ROAD MAP TO JOY

Scripture
"For it stands in Scripture: 'Behold, I am laying in Zion a stone, a cornerstone chosen and precious, and whoever believes in him will not be put to shame'" (1 Pet. 2:6, ESV).

Prayer
Dear Lord, I thank You for Your death on the cross of Calvary and what it means for me as a believer in this life and the life to come.

Activation
If you have never gazed into the bloody wounds and scars of Jesus, never remembered His death and suffering, then you are in for a bittersweet revelation. Take time this week to study and meditate daily on verses surrounding Jesus' death. Take time to ponder the price He paid to give you a new and eternal life. Embracing, rather than turning away from, the painful death of Jesus will cause your spirit to break in wonderful ways, releasing new joy, perspective, and a greater measure of the Holy Spirit.

If you are Jewish and have rejected Jesus as the long-awaited Messiah, take the time to read Isaiah 53, remembering the pure lamb offered at Passover. This lamb is the Lamb of God, who bled and died for the sins of Jews and gentiles alike. His name in Hebrew is Yeshua, or "salvation." It is natural for you to ask God to give you a sign that He is the one true God in the form of Jesus. He will reveal Himself to you.

Further Study
1 Peter 2:8, 1 Corinthians 2:2, and Galatians 5:11

Recommended Reading
The Glory and the Shame: Reflections on the 20th-Century Outpouring of the Holy Spirit by Peter D. Hocken, and *Restoring the Jewishness of the Gospel: A Message for Christians* by David H. Stern

White blossoms shining and upturned; soft petal faces scrubbed clean in sunlight.

Healing

God whispers to us in our pleasure, speaks in our conscience, but shouts in our pain: it is His megaphone to rouse a deaf world.
—C. S. Lewis

T he river of disappointment
and sorrow—the one that catches
in your throat and that you swallow

back. The one that stings your eyes
hot with betraying tears—if you
release that pain to stream

freely, it will push out, out to
empty itself into the vast deep
of the salty ocean brine

that scrubs clean the wound. Then
only a faint scar remains and gleams
just under the wash of lapping, laughing

waves and silent sunshine. Now go home
and close your eyes, remember letting go
and feeling weightless—and yes, the ocean

turned to blood for a second, and
the deadwood that you clutched
floated back out to the sea.

ROAD MAP TO JOY

Healing the trauma of abuse, neglect, or abandonment (the list goes on and on) is a lifetime endeavor. Sometimes, though, healing can come suddenly through the help of a counselor, a trusted friend, a prayer, an enlightened scripture, or a worship service. When you ask God to help you with life's bruises, He will make a way for deliverance. The process has been both quick and slow in my life—truly a journey of healing. I wrote this poem when I began to come alive—when I realized a vast measure of my pain had been deeply healed. The first signs of renewal began as the will to resist spiraling toxic thoughts, and then I replaced them with thanksgiving—not for the hurt but for the good that God was creating from the disappointments. I didn't fear seeing the people that had hurt me but instead embraced them! It was a miracle. I had setbacks, of course, but kept pushing forward into pools of forgiveness, centering on a scripture, that God works all things for my good (Rom. 8:28). Joy returned to me in double, and streams of trust in God's ability to heal fully continued to flow around this new gift of restoration. I can never stop thanking God for mending my broken heart, and caressing and healing life's hidden bruises.

Scripture
"You keep track of all my sorrows. You have collected all my tears in your bottle. You have recorded each one in your book. My enemies will retreat when I call to you for help. This I know: God is on my side" (Ps. 56:8–9, NLT).

Prayer
Thank You, Lord, for taking bruises on Your body so that my inner bruises and trauma can be healed, my life forever changed. I ask that You heal me thoroughly and completely as I continue this process.

Activation
We all have inner wounds, and sometimes, seeking help beyond ourselves is necessary and beneficial. My husband and I have both seen a counselor, together and separately, for the hurts and scars of life. If you have trauma that occasionally brings painful or toxic

memories, pray about getting professional help or counsel from someone who can help you overcome the bruises of life. This will restore or replenish your joy.

Further Study
2 Kings 20:5, Psalm 39:12, and Malachi 3:16

Recommended Reading
Who Switched Off My Brain?: Controlling Toxic Thoughts and Emotions by Dr. Caroline Leaf, and *The Way of the Heart: Connecting with God Through Faith* by Henri J. M. Nouwen

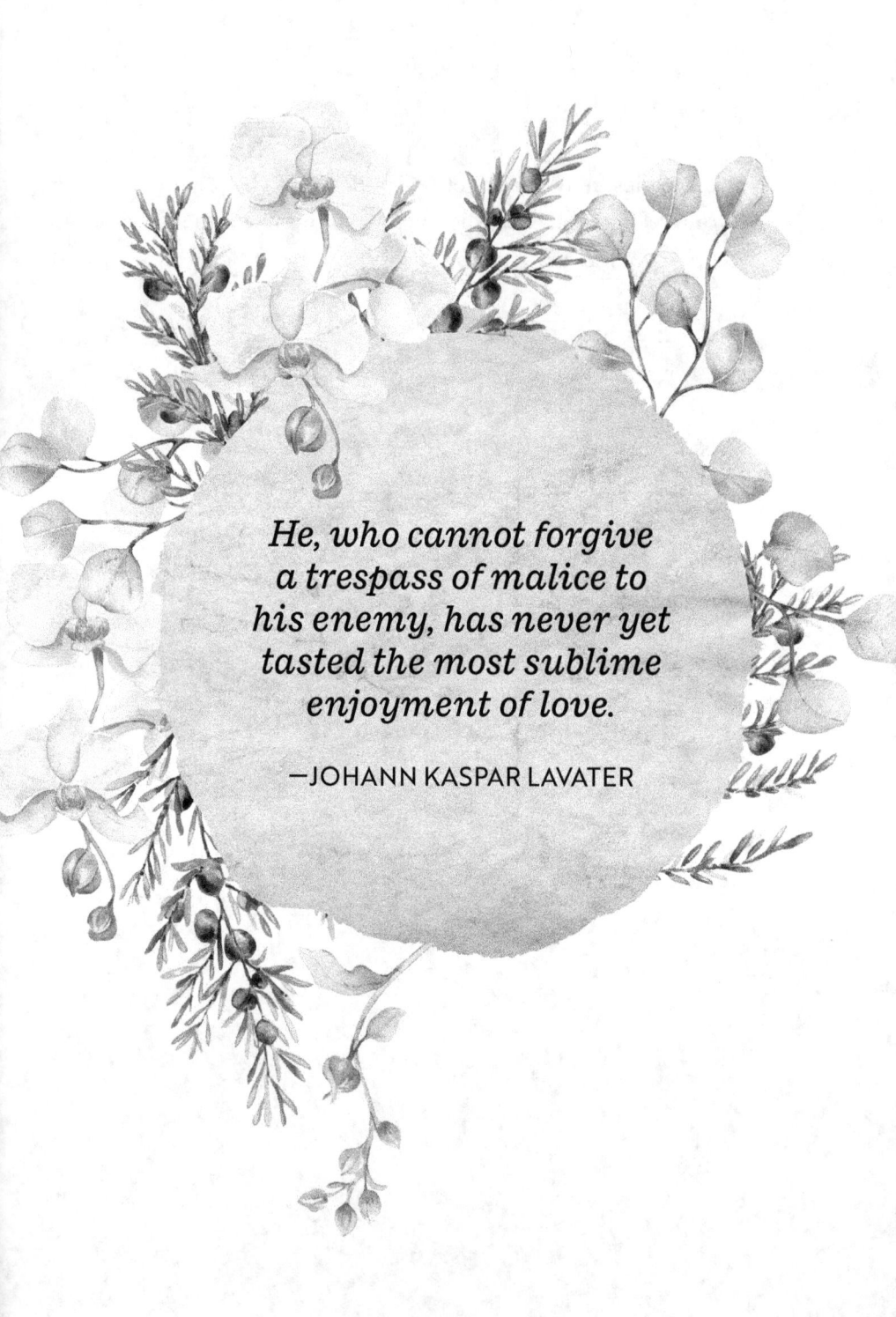

He, who cannot forgive a trespass of malice to his enemy, has never yet tasted the most sublime enjoyment of love.

—JOHANN KASPAR LAVATER

Table of Forgiveness

> You prepare a table before me in the presence of my enemies. You anoint my head with oil; my cup overflows.
> —*Psalm 23:5*

A myriad of memories flashing across my mind, this scripture sprang into living color. When Wayne and I lived in Israel, we made numerous trips to the desert. Amid the arid, uncultivable hills and valleys, God faithfully spoke to us. Sometimes we drove for miles along the Dead Sea in silence, watching the light and shadow play on the rough terrain. We knew from experience that in the quiet waiting, God would speak direction, encouragement, or even correction. And how appropriate! Even the Hebrew word for *desert*, *midbar* (מִדְבָּר), contains the root "to speak."

I, a world citizen of the early twenty-first century, have suffered the onslaught of epic death and loss with the pandemic, cultural wars, shifting societal morals, cancel culture, and betrayal. Even with cleansed and renewed vision daily, my eyes still see a howling wasteland stretched before me, one of suffering and injustice. Once, I asked myself, "When will this end?" The Lord spoke to me immediately—in this cultural wilderness, He is setting a table before me in the presence of my enemies, and He fills my cup to overflow.

As He spoke, I imagined myself at a long, wooden table amid the desolation of broken lives, death, irrevocable change, and instability. The Lord asked, "Your table is long and empty—why not invite your enemies to sit with you?"

I sat stunned. Enemies?

He continued, "Your cup overflows—so you have plenty to share."

I don't like the idea of having enemies. It sounds weak or like I have unresolved issues. God forbid. But one by one, the chairs around my table began to fill. The faces surprised me, many I didn't even know personally. Somehow, through the horrific and unconscionable events of the last decade, I built walls and created villains while trying to navigate the shock and suffering we all endured. At that moment, most of my enemies were people I would never meet but who had deeply influenced my life by their decisions.

I imagined each offense, forgiving or asking for forgiveness. The tears poured. I realized that some were truly not enemies but individuals I could blame when things careen out of control.

I shifted my vision from the temporal to the eternal and knew God is truly over all events. This was a cleansing exercise for me, one I plan to repeat from time to time.

I know the circumstances and faces at the table will change—somehow the generous act of forgiveness is never finished in this life.

I'm embracing the promises of God fully, for I know I will be forgiven as I forgive.

ROAD MAP TO JOY

Scripture
"For if you forgive other people when they sin against you, your heavenly Father will also forgive you" (Matt. 6:14).

Prayer
Dear Lord, give me the mercy, courage, and faith to forgive others as You have forgiven me.

Activation
Metaphorically (or literally, if appropriate), invite your enemies to dine with you. You may be surprised at who shows up and the length of your table. Choose to forgive, leaving justice and vengeance to God. Journal about it. The experience may become a treasured wellspring from which you can routinely draw strength and courage. Few things in life fill your heart with joy like deep and sincere forgiveness.

Further Study
Ephesians 4:32, Mark 11:25, and Colossians 3:13

Recommended Reading
The Hiding Place by Corrie ten Boom, and *God's Smuggler* by Brother Andrew, John Sherrill, and Elizabeth Sherrill

A pleasure is only full-grown when it is remembered.

—C. S. LEWIS

Quiet Morning

In our midlives, the time when most begin to think about retiring someday, God called us to the mission field. We had a lovely home, and Wayne had a fulfilling job. But after fourteen years of serving in ministry and leading short-term mission trips, God fulfilled our dream to serve the Jewish people in Eastern Europe.

Tearfully we said goodbye to family and friends and boarded a plane for Ukraine. After twenty-four hours, multiple flights, and several connections, the small Wilks family of three arrived in the former Soviet Union.

We rented a small village house with a well and grape arbor. That first night, we fell into bed feeling exhausted in a strange, new place. The phone didn't work, the electricity was out, and the water wasn't running, so we had to dip in the well to drink. We could not bathe for one week—I know, it sounds horrific. Welcome to life outside of the United States.

Our new life was baptism by fire, burning off the comforts of home through culture, language learning, and strange food and customs. We didn't know our neighbors and prayed they would like us—or at least help us.

The airline left our luggage and two cats in their carriers in the rain, so our clothes arrived soaked, and the cats were cold, wet, and totally freaked out. Well, they weren't alone. I was concerned the cats would get sick; they had been left wet in the cold cargo part of the plane for twenty-four hours. No wonder they did not purr for thirty days after arriving!

On top of that, our landlords had not moved out—their personal belongings filled the kitchen cabinets, bedroom closets, and drawers. Later, we were told this is customary; renters should just "move their stuff over" to make room. What a shock! I looked around and wondered if I could live like this for the next five to ten years.

Our first morning, while Wayne and Julia still slept, I awoke in the village house—friends, family, and memories behind us, and new adventures and friends before us.

I brewed a cup of coffee and opened my journal. The sweet morning light shone through the window.

With all the uncertainty and strangeness, my heart settled into the kind of peace only God can give when there is lack of human understanding and comfort.

I didn't know what would happen next; I just knew God had prepared us and would take care of us. I wrote this poem in those very first moments of our new beginning.

QUIET MORNING

Puzzle pieces of morning light
gleam through thin kitchen curtains.

Outside, plump ruby grapes dangle
from twisted vines and

vibrant grape leaves
hang motionless

in the still of first light.
My soul is as peaceful

as the Ukrainian morning.
I read and drink coffee

in the humble kitchen of
stout-hearty Soviet friends.

Their rickety kitchen table
jiggles as I journal.

A half-eaten grape cluster
leans against a chunk of

yesterday's crusty brown bread.
My heart sings and swells for

simplicity, for quiet. Distant
jagged patterns and neon colors

of home emerge:
grasping for Ralph Lauren,

clawing for Vera Wang,
force-feeding the fat,

rescuing the apathetic,
competing, running in the

left lane winded, jaded,
gathering with both fists full.

This home-scene memory
rushes before my eyes vividly,

but I can't hear it.
The morning is too quiet.

ROAD MAP TO JOY

I remember feeling afraid of the future in a strange land but not so fearful I'd stay home. On the first day, I could tell this new life would be harder than I had imagined. Still, God met me in my frailty and offered the pleasures of a beautiful morning, coffee, homemade bread, a safe place to stay, and a good reason to push forward into the unknown. I will treasure the memory of that first morning in Ukraine.

Living in the former Soviet Union, I had to develop new eyes to recognize a different kind of pleasure. My senses remained on high alert as I learned to adapt and thrive in a barren setting. This pursuit brought overflowing joy, quiet, and gratefulness.

Scripture
"All the days of the oppressed are wretched, but the cheerful heart has a continual feast" (Prov. 15:15).

Prayer

I thank You, Lord, for the small things that bring me comfort and pleasure. Your provision is remarkable.

Activation

Only you decide how your life will shine and thrive in barren places. Choose a grateful heart. Choose cheerfulness. Choose loving little pleasures. Turn dry breadcrumbs into chocolate-chip cookies. It will restore and maintain your joy.

Further Study

1 Thessalonians 5:18, Colossians 3:17, and Psalm 107:1

Recommended Reading

Simple Joys: Discovering Wonder in the Everyday by Candace Payne, and *The Joy of Fearing God* by Jerry Bridges

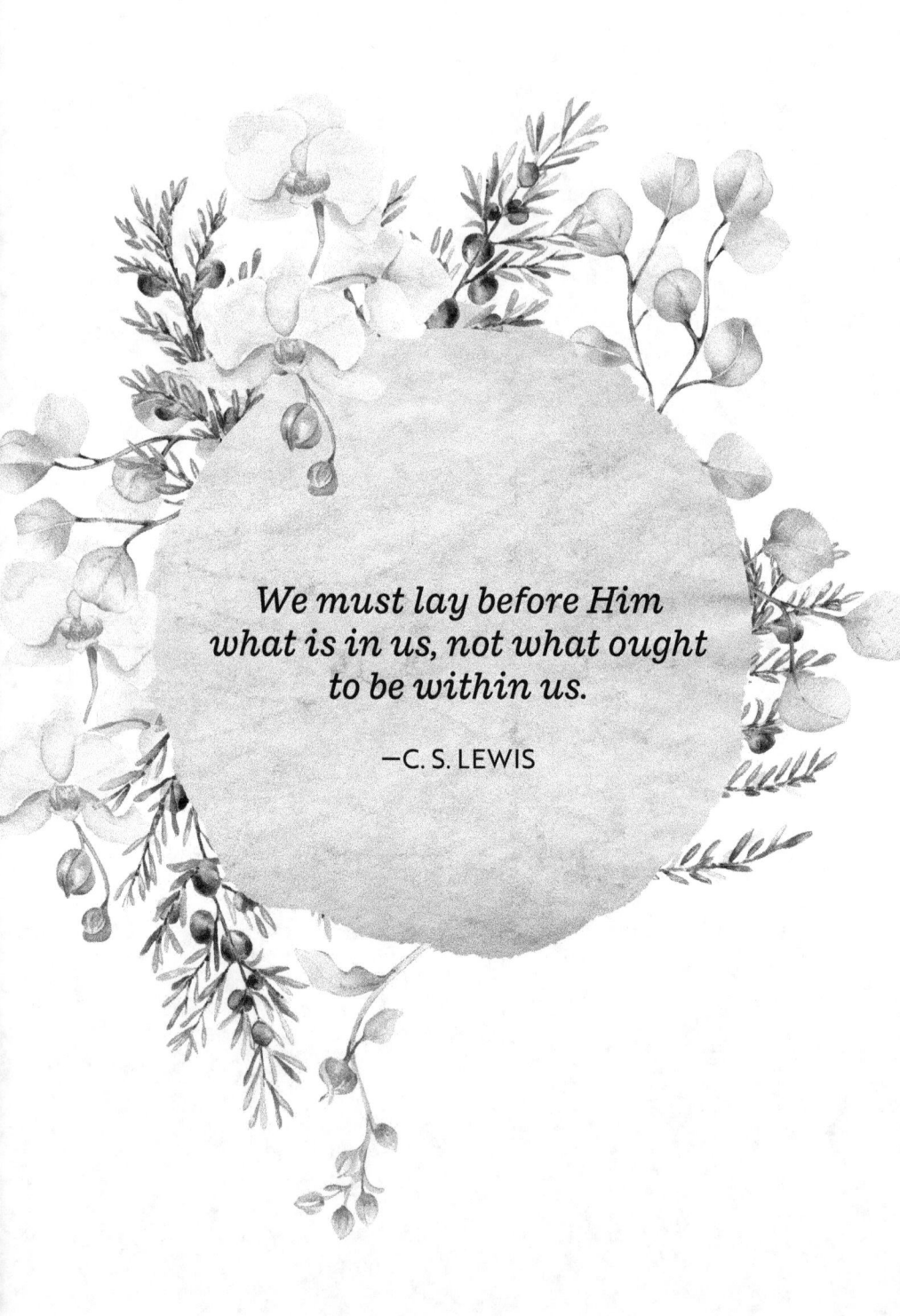

10

One Nod

In time, you stop gathering things and begin to collect moments.
You learn to draw a deep furrowed line in the world to hedge off the chaos and begin to measure life by the wealth of blessing

without sorrow and suffering that has turned evil for good.
At long last, you cease competition and cleave to the unseen world.
Hardship enables you to give out of your desperate need, to inspire

and comfort instead of underscoring and highlighting achievements.
With reverence, you embrace the obscurity of hiddenness, silence,

and waiting. At last, you hold nothing back to return to
the beginning

without thought of losing ground. Tears fall and
the heart swells
with gratitude because you know that it's always
been about the
blinding darkness of Calvary and the unapproachable
light of an empty

tomb—neatly folded grave clothes found in that
obscure garden,
and your trembling ascent to obedience and significant calling.
It's always been about one nod of approval that you
could never earn.

ROAD MAP TO JOY

I've always been a people pleaser, and this took me down a few very crazy and joyless pathways. Honestly, it became exhausting. It took years to learn that people-pleasing is an unending, relentless, and often fruitless adventure. The warm love and unconditional acceptance from my Father above is the only nod of approval I need. Whoever I am trying to please becomes my master, and the apostle Paul makes it clear that believers cannot serve two bosses. Life still brings me the choice almost daily. The Holy Spirit is faithful to guide me and give me the grace to choose wisely. When I know I am making my Savior happy by endeavoring to make Him the center of my life, joy runs deep.

Scripture
"Am I now trying to win the approval of human beings, or of God? Or am I trying to please people? If I were still trying to please people, I would not be a servant of Christ" (Gal. 1:10).

Prayer
I thank You, Lord, for bringing me into a relationship with You through Your death and resurrection on the cross. May this supreme sacrifice inspire and motivate me to seek Your approval alone.

Activation
Ask the Holy Spirit to nudge you when you find yourself running in circles, trying to please others. Ask Him to show you the root cause of seeking the approval of others rather than God. Reset your focus on your heavenly Father's approval. Freedom from people-pleasing to seeking God brings great joy.

Further Study
1 Thessalonians 2:4, Acts 5:29, and Ephesians 6:6

Recommended Reading
The Approval Fix: How to Break Free from People Pleasing by Joyce Meyer, and *Dealing with the Rejection and Praise of Man* by Bob Sorge

I was broken before I was broken. This shattering of my soul has shaken me awake to see it.

11

Gold Glue

To be a Christian means to forgive the inexcusable, because God has forgiven the inexcusable in you.
—C. S. Lewis

A dear friend from Chile brought me a gift from her hometown of Santiago. I unwrapped the pretty box to find a blue-and-white porcelain, intricately carved heart with a lid, designed to hold small pieces of jewelry. I loved it immediately and appreciated the kind thoughtfulness. It sat on my bedroom dresser for years.

When we moved to a new house, the delicate porcelain piece slipped from my hands and broke—a clean and simple break—it was easy to repair with glue. Some years later it broke again into more pieces, but amazingly I glued it once more! It now had a tiny, unfixable chip, and the glued cracks became wider and more visible, but I still treasured the gift.

Sadly, through miscommunication and misunderstanding, Wayne and I had a different friendship fall apart. Later, after months of separation, accusations, and heartache, we came together to work on mending and reconciling our relationship. Eventually we both asked for forgiveness and moved forward, leaving the pain in the past.

Years later I went to lunch with the same friend and gave her the broken and mended porcelain heart as a gift. I handed the cracked and repaired offering to her, explaining it symbolized our friendship—broken and repaired many times over. Despite our selfish foolishness, we still held together through unconditional and forgiving love. I'll never forget the touching moment.

I thought the falling out broke both of us, but in truth, we were already broken. We started our friendship with bruised spirits, life already shattering us before we met. That stony path of friendship caused us to trip over the scattered rocks of offense—ones we should've stepped over with love and patience. I realized how every relationship can lead to a deeper break if we begin in an already crushed state.

Brokenness reveals brokenness.

Sometimes you must break completely before you can be healed and brought to wholeness.

The Japanese have a technique called *kintsugi*, where they repair broken vessels by soldering them together with liquid gold. The vessels become more precious after being broken and mended because it makes them stronger and more beautiful.

Brokenness is a beautiful quality and certainly something I look for now in relationships. It has the power to heal, bring us to our knees, allow us to see the reality of who we are and learn to offer others mercy. When we humbly yield our rights and respond with tenderness, those moments can become opportunities to gather the broken pieces—bringing them to God in prayer and to those we've hurt through our unholiness. The fruit of forgiveness and reconciliation is the sweetest gift!

Jesus was the only human who didn't start broken. But He chose to break when He willingly gave His life and suffered for our healing and salvation. He yielded His life to put us back together.

I can still picture the porcelain heart I offered my friend—all the broken pieces and glue holding it together. I can still see her face as I explained—both of us thankful for second, third, and fourth chances in life. Forgiveness will continue forever, until we kiss the scarred hands and feet of the master mender of hearts. I'm so glad the shattering of life can be filled with His goodness—the gold glue of redeeming love. Only God can turn my brokenness into beauty and restore joy.

ROAD MAP TO JOY

Scriptures
"He heals the brokenhearted and binds up their wounds" (Ps. 147:3).

"Bear with each other and forgive one another if any of you have a grievance against someone. Forgive as the Lord forgave you" (Col. 3:13).

Prayer
I thank You, Lord, for forgiving me and giving me new life and second chances. Please give me the courage and power to forgive those who have offended me.

Activation
In conflict, often both parties are at fault, but sometimes there is only one party responsible for the grievance. No matter. To seek reconciliation, the ultimate goal of forgiveness, you must be comfortable with the possibility of never fully understanding all viewpoints.

It is possible to forgive deeply and reconcile without coming to agreement about the conflict. Ask God to show you how to approach the person and what to say to reconcile and bring restitution. If the break in the relationship is severe, consider using a mediator to help resolve the conflict. It can bring great relief and freedom to everyone involved. Nothing restores your joy as the reconciliation of broken relationships.

Further Study
Ephesians 4:32, Mark 11:25, and James 2:13

Recommended Reading
Free of Charge: Giving and Forgiving in a Culture Stripped of Grace by Miroslav Volf, and *Forgiving as We've Been Forgiven: Community Practices for Making Peace* by L. Gregory Jones and Célestin Musekura

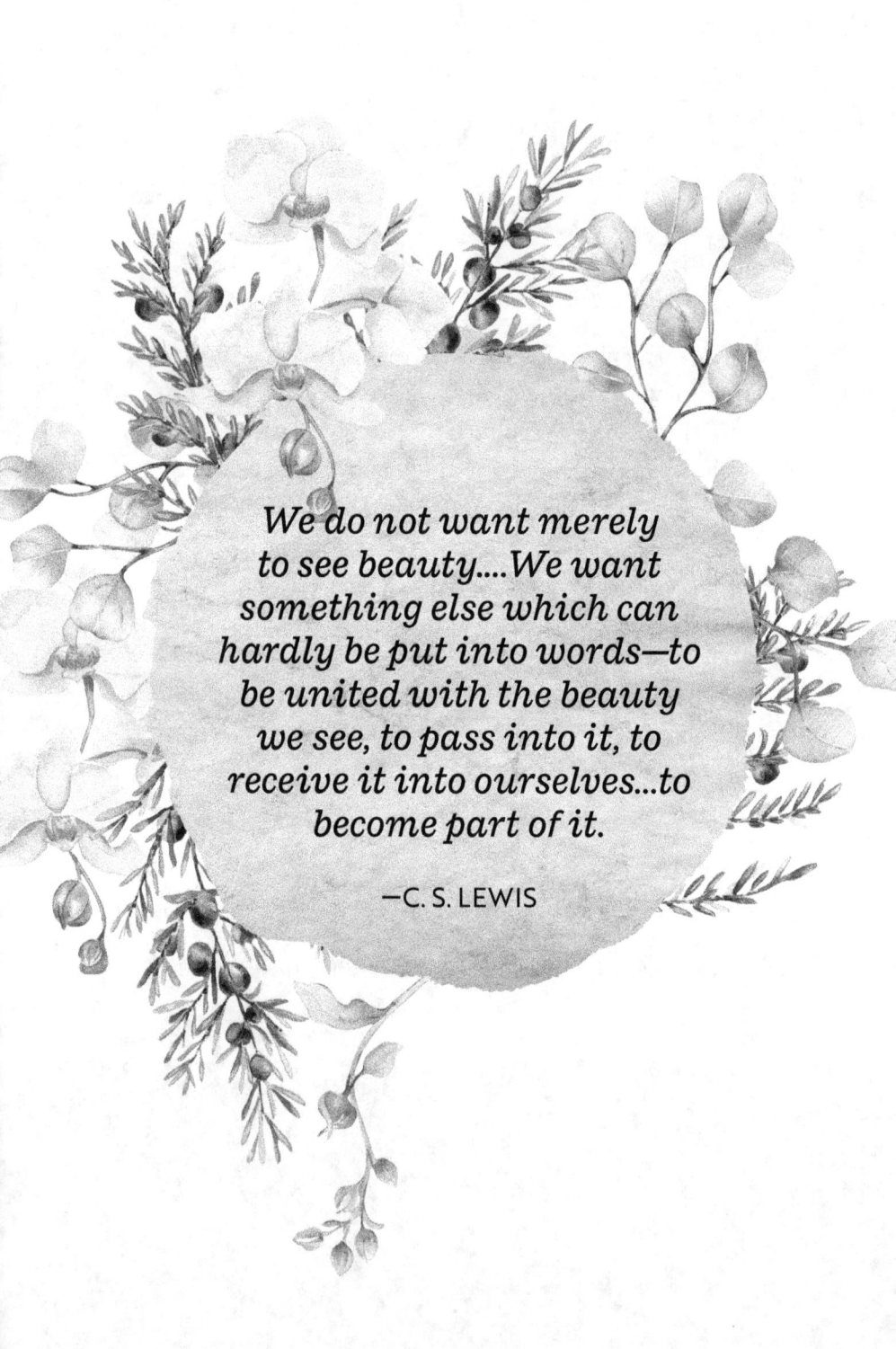

We do not want merely to see beauty....We want something else which can hardly be put into words—to be united with the beauty we see, to pass into it, to receive it into ourselves...to become part of it.

—C. S. LEWIS

12

Rusted Filigrees

It will not be said of me that "I staggered not" at the
promises of faith, rather that "my hand held the sword."
I've altered and swayed, plummeted in despair, and
hoped to hope; yet I held focus, in all the shifting, on Him

that changes not. I've lingered much on rusted filigrees
and the crushed fragments of carved columns.
Finding beauty in every place is a gift that
should slow you down.

Squeeze between the sheets of a thin place,
there you will find
the comfort of the eternal; there you will brush
with that which

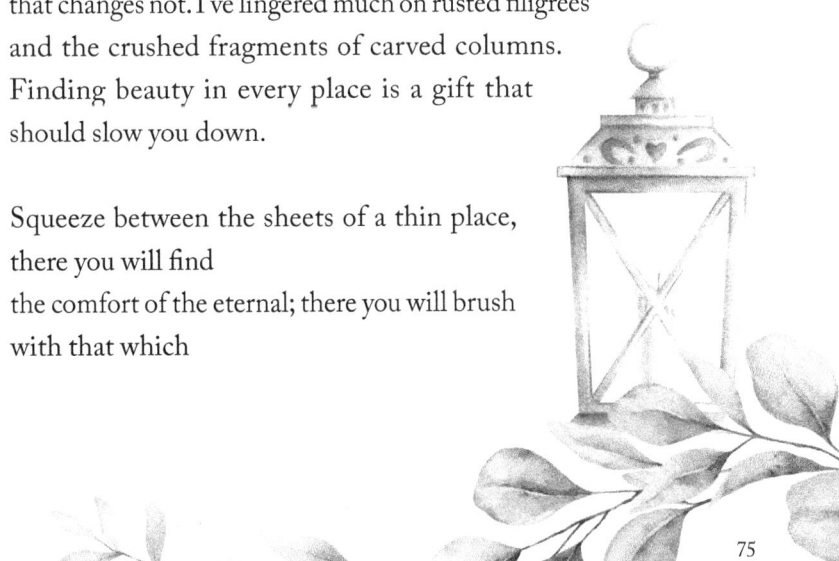

is holy and defines purpose today and beyond. There, in the narrow
space, you will ask questions that will change you forever and

lend meaning to the mundane, like will the deep tracks that I leave—
will they be at the stovetop or glued to a computer, in front of a mirror, or buckled into a jet seat flying over the sea or counting the petals of a velvet, pink rose? The widow and orphan,

the blind and starved are the royalty of this old earth. Linger long, long on these. Leave oil for their scars, buckets of living water for thirst, baskets of bread for hunger, and packets of seeds— and more packets of seeds for tomorrow's planting.

ROAD MAP TO JOY

Writing a poem is like starting on a journey whose end is unknown. It is always an adventure. I began this poem with one of my favorite Scriptures in mind:

> He arose, and smote the Philistines until his hand was weary, and his hand clave unto the sword; and the Lord wrought a great victory that day; and the people returned after him only to spoil.
> —2 Samuel 23:10, kjv

From the time I read this verse, I was smitten. Even as a teenager, courage rose within me to stay vigilant and fight life's battles, even when weary. This sounds so lofty! It took years to figure out the costly price for this kind of commitment—to stay the course of war until the battle is won. Some days I lose more battles than I win. It takes years of warfare to develop the mental and physical strength to persevere in good faith.

The poem ends by embracing both the joy and sorrow of the journey—celebrating the beauty found between life's battles and the hope of leaving something eternal behind. Here's to the faith, stamina, and fortitude it takes to cleave to the sword during the intensity of war and all that lies beyond earth's fleeting moments of the battleground.

Scripture
"I have fought the good fight, I have finished the race, I have kept the faith" (2 Tim. 4:7).

Prayer
Dear Lord, please grant me the strength and fortitude to cleave to following and obeying You through all of life's battles. May my legacy be that "my hand clave to the sword."

Activation
Reflect on your life. Ask the Lord if there are battles you fought but gave up in defeat. If so, inquire more—some wars are not worth the effort, and others are. Ask for the Lord's wisdom to revisit pertinent old battles with new eyes and the ability to stay faithful in the things God requires of you.

Further Study
Ephesians 6:10–18, 2 Corinthians 4:5, and Romans 15:18

Recommended Reading
Fervent: A Woman's Battle Plan for Serious, Specific, and Strategic Prayer by Priscilla Shirer, and *The Screwtape Letters* by C. S. Lewis

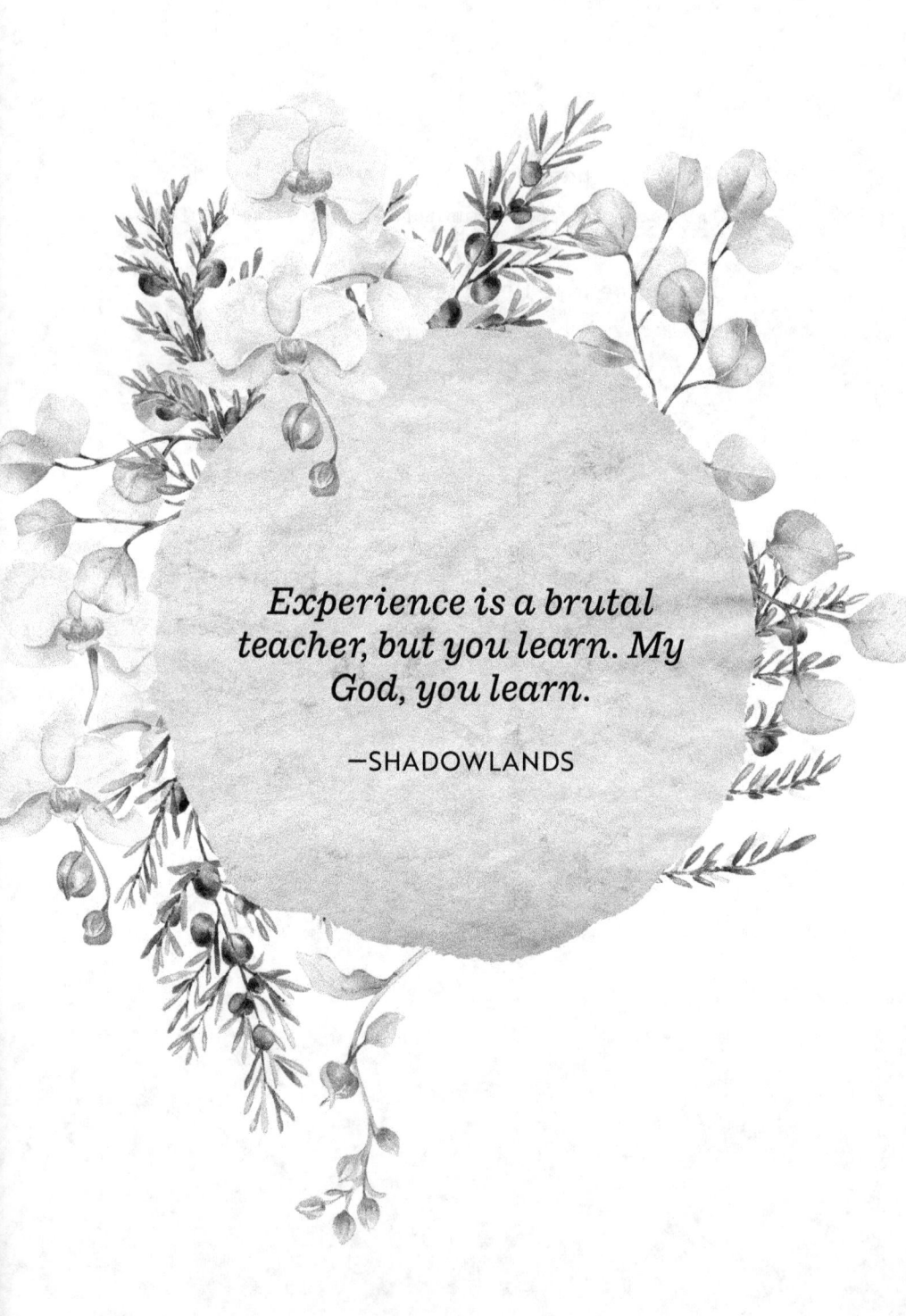

Experience is a brutal teacher, but you learn. My God, you learn.

—SHADOWLANDS

13

Desert Purple

I used to be a very sad person. At age twenty-four I attempted suicide—something I am certainly not proud of, but I can boast of the redeeming power of God, which turned my mourning into dancing and darkness into light.

I remember waking up in a psychiatric hospital after a few nightmarish happenings. The events of the previous months were blurry; I just knew I wanted to die. I felt hopeless. My mom sat by my bed with love and steadiness the night my world collapsed; she told me that she and my dad loved me, no matter what—I felt their love.

I asked for a Bible the next day. I remember looking at myself in the mirror, thinking I never wanted to comb my hair again.

I started to read my Bible with sad but new eyes. Even though I had been raised in a Christian home where I understood salvation, I never quite understood how to stand against depression or negative and toxic thought patterns.

Inner healing came but ever so slowly—it took two years of therapy and recalibrating my life. I pressed into God and His Word. Hope and light filled my life as I saw myself as God sees me, with a "future and a hope" (Jer. 29:11, NKJV).

During the barren desert of my life, Jesus stayed close and helped me through. My favorite scripture during my recovery was Song of Songs 8:5: "Who is this that comes up from the wilderness leaning on her beloved?"

In that isolated, dark time I learned that God wants intimacy with His people in the dry places in life. I learned that His love for me was so deep and sweet, and it satisfies like nothing else. Sometimes He leads us into the wilderness so we will become stripped of our own abilities and dependency on others to fully cling to Him. Yes, even as Scripture says, leaning on Him as we heal from our suffering.

That experience made me appreciate the real desert—to see its beauty and know it symbolizes intimacy with my beloved Redeemer and Creator like nothing else. Desert colors intrigue and captivate me. I had always thought of the wasted, dry places of the earth as being brown, beige, and browner. It is interesting to discover there is a lot of purple in the desert. I love the surprise of that—the incongruity of that.

Purple throughout the Scriptures means royalty or wealth. Kings and the wealthy could afford purple garments, which were dyed with expensive additives from sea animals. Exodus describes the Tabernacle of Moses as having ten linen curtains dyed purple, blue, and scarlet. There were angels embroidered on them of the same hues. In Acts the wealthy woman Lydia sold purple. There was also the rich man in Luke who wore purple. And in the book of Mark, Jesus

Himself wore a purple garment when He was mocked and ridiculed before He was crucified.

In dreams purple symbolizes royalty, symbolizes something heavenly, or points to deity. It has supernatural meaning, something beyond the here and now. I always pay attention to purple. Colors have powerful meanings spiritually, so to find such an abundance of purple in the desert took my breath away. Who can know all the things God is speaking to us by His artistic, creative paintings left in the plant life of the desert?

One of the most significant things about when the bride of Christ arises from the wilderness is she is not recognized by her peers as being the same person. She has been so changed by the love of God in her time of suffering her friends ask, "Who is this that comes up from the wilderness leaning on her beloved?"

Like the bride in the wilderness, I emerged from my dry, desert experience totally different. In fact, I have never returned to that place again. I have never considered suicide, and I am rarely ever depressed. Truly the Lord Jesus has turned my mourning into dancing.

I descended into the desert to taste death and discovered that Jesus tasted death for every man. Now I will not live a life eternally separated from God. My life is just the opposite: I am living in close, even intimate, relationship with the God of the universe. He made me beautiful through the desert. When I was unlovely and undesirable, He desired me. I emerged from the desert place as Christ's beloved—clothed in purple and precious to Him.

ROAD MAP TO JOY

I love desert purple. It points to something higher taking place when we bow low and walk through difficult times. Desert purple is God's door of hope, reminding us there is something significant, eternal, and lovely beyond the dusty path of death we walk.

Scripture
"Therefore I am now going to allure her; I will lead her into the wilderness and speak tenderly to her. There I will give her back her vineyards, and I will make the Valley of Achor a door of hope" (Hos. 2:14–15).

Prayer
Dear Lord, help me remember that sometimes You allow the dry, desert places to help us know Your love and care more intimately and to strengthen and stretch our faith. Help me to embrace this place and give me gratitude and joy in endurance.

Activation
Perhaps you are walking through a wilderness of heartache or disappointments, which really tests your faith. Remember God's faithfulness in the desert place. Press in, expressing gratitude to God, family, friends, and coworkers more profusely. Keep yourself watered by clinging to the precious Scriptures God has given that produce an overcoming life. Joy runs deep in the desert place when you find the true source of living water.

Further Study
Isaiah 40:3, Psalm 107:2–8, and Jeremiah 2:2

Recommended Reading
The Dance of Life: Weaving Sorrows and Blessings into One Joyful Step by Henri J. M. Nouwen, and *The Scandal of the Kingdom: How the Parables of Jesus Revolutionize Life with God* by Dallas Willard

Blood red flowers burst from the cold earth, healing hidden scars that winter left.

14

At the Nail Salon

Has the world been so kind to you that you should leave with regret? There are better things ahead than any we leave behind.
—C. S. Lewis

Although everyone I know loves the luxuries of a manicure, pedicure, or facial, I do not. The truth is, I never had a pedicure or facial without the scolding of the professional offering her skills. Apparently, I've done an inadequate job managing my feet or face on my own.

Can you relate?

Since we're on the subject, I've rarely seen a dentist, doctor, or chiropractor who didn't shame or scare me into good health. You see, professional people—I much prefer to be comforted, affirmed, and inspired to do better, not scolded or shamed.

What I am really sharing here is the result of childhood emotional wounds that pop up in the oddest places, like the local dentistry or nail salon.

With these experiences, there is always regret edging its way in too. I have seen it in my mother and father's gazes as they have grown old and longed to connect with their children as adults more openly and intimately. The welling up of pain and the irrevocable swift passing of time pools in their eyes and runs warm down the soft skin of their cheeks. I have blinked away my own pained regrets with my daughter.

In every generation there is no new brokenness under the sun, sky, or stars at night. We step over and on the shattered fragments of people's pain every day. But today, I gazed into my granddaughter's eyes and saw the clean slate of fresh hope in a new generation and the healing power of love through the simple wisdom of living long enough to know regret.

Childhood bruises are swallowed up forever in one big gulp of forgiveness and a thousand tiny kindnesses and kisses every day ever after. The ground under my feet swells with purpose as I age, and I run with light feet now loaded with bags and bags of mercy to give as I have been given.

Mercy mending, connecting, and stitching the generations together as a scarlet banner signaling to the world, "This is a safe place."

That we may be safe.
Oh, the blood and water that courses through the earth from Jerusalem's Calvary that we may be safe.

ROAD MAP TO JOY

I married later in life, at the age of thirty-two, and I fondly recall that first year as glorious. Besides the wonders of a new life together, I began to spill my childhood trauma to my husband. As I sat on his lap and poured out pain in his loving arms, I found healing and unconditional acceptance. Unfolding events and expressing the hurt brought great emotional freedom. Later, I saw several counselors and received professional help. Two keys that have worked for me over and over as I sought wholeness were developing a lifestyle of gratefulness and forgiveness. When I take the smallest, maybe painful steps toward these attributes, God meets me and grants renewal and hope.

Scripture
"But if we walk in the light, as he is in the light, we have fellowship with one another, and the blood of Jesus, his Son, purifies us from all sin" (1 John 1:7).

Prayer
Dear Lord, I bring my childhood or adult trauma to You and ask You to heal me. Bring me wholeness so my actions toward those around me will not perpetuate the sins or mistakes of previous generations.

Activation
As believers we are called to reconciliation. What areas need repair and reconciliation in your life due to trauma? Make a list. Make it a serious matter of prayer. Ask God for answers. God has a solution for deep heart healing—the sins and mistakes of others in your life or previous generations don't have to continue to hurt or harm you.

Further Study
Ephesians 5:8, Revelation 1:5, and Romans 13:12

Recommended Reading
It Didn't Start with You: How Inherited Family Trauma Shapes Who We Are and How to End the Cycle by Mark Wolynn, and *The Body Keeps the Score: Brain, Mind, and Body in the Healing of Trauma* by Bessel Van Der Kolk, MD

15
Lavender Shirt Not Required

Leaning against the wooden porch fence in his crisp lavender shirt and black dress pants at the wayside barbecue, the Texas cowboy explained that he'd just come from the church up the road. With a zest for life, the man spoke about local news and history while we stood in line for our Sunday supper takeout. Then, stepping forward with a bounce, the boyish man announced that he was eighty-five and not retired.

We gasped. Incredible! I wanted to connect with him more.

Since he'd just come from church, I asked his favorite scripture. With animation and childlike wonder, he quipped, "It's hard to choose—what about you?"

"For God so loved the world that he gave his only begotten son that whosoever believes in him should not perish but have eternal life," I answered.

With bright, dancing eyes, he continued, "For God sent not his son into the world to condemn the world, but that the world through him might be saved."

Then the man stepped forward and handed me a tract—a simple, colorful explanation of salvation.

The greatest gift.

I accepted it.

Oh, the kinship of fellow soldiers, fellow disciples.

Not remarkable or wealthy by worldly standards, this man's life stood out, overflowing with joy and hope for the future. His choices poured joy, hope, and strength into my journey.

The pathway leading to life abundant and heavenly gates—escaping the flame of hell—is simple but unrelentingly narrow.

Lavender shirts are not required. Eventually, you must retrieve the tract from the trash bin where you tossed it after receiving it, and read it.

ROAD MAP TO JOY

Scripture
"But you will receive power when the Holy Spirit has come upon you; and you shall be my witnesses in Jerusalem, and in all Judea and Samaria, and to the ends of the earth" (Acts 1:8).

Prayer
Dear Lord, I ask for a fresh infilling of the Holy Spirit so I have boldness to share the good news of the gospel. If I have not done so, I ask for the grace to receive the message of Christ's sacrifice for me.

Activation
Practice sharing your testimony of how God has changed your life. Have a one-, two-, or five-minute presentation

prepared. Sometimes you don't have that long, and in the swift-running world of sound bites, people have even less patience to listen. Knowing what to say when the opportunity arrives will deescalate the fear of stepping out. Sharing the new life that God has given through His Son will bring rivers of joy to your spirit and soul.

Further Study
Mark 16:15, Acts 2:38–39, and Luke 24:47–48

Recommended Reading
Evangelism by Fire: Keys for Effectively Reaching Others with the Gospel by Reinhard Bonnke, and *Power Evangelism* by John Wimber and Kevin Springer

The lion's share of faith is gratefulness.

The Pandemic

> We are not necessarily doubting that God will do the best for us: we are wondering how painful the best will turn out to be.
> —C. S. Lewis

We buried the dead for months and then years, and we mourned, wept, and waited for it to pass. Some prayed, and some railed. Others burned and

some stole. Some legislated, and some pressed on. Some died, and some lived. Some shouted into the dark, and others escaped the flames.

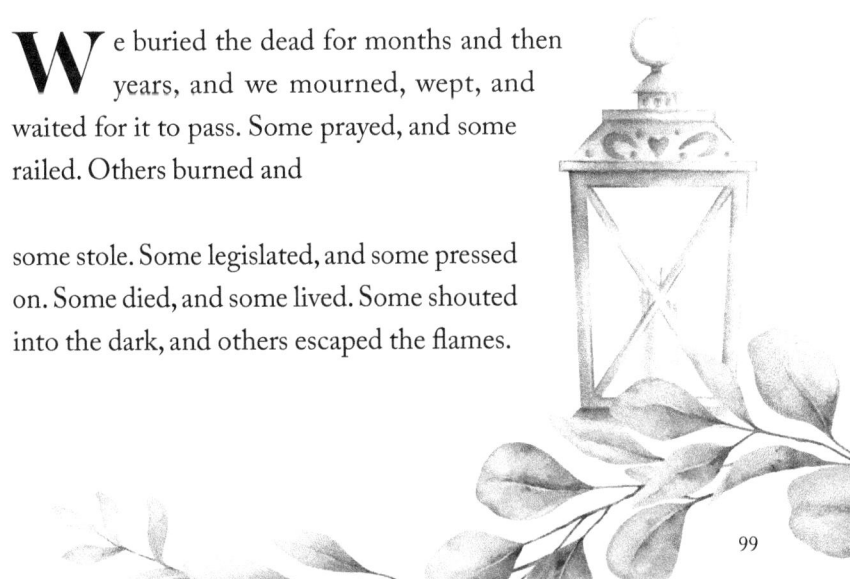

Everyone's hair was singed. Each looked for someone to blame, but they told us, never mind, it was bad from the start. We tried to come back—

to live again, but the divide grew and threatened to split us apart—America. We stood with one foot on different continents in our hometowns. The

shifting societal norms made us stand crooked, and rising to walk, we limped. We limped forward and fell backward. This morning, I watched

widows weep and saw the fatherless children lean in to their mothers' scant shadows. There is a place lower than the grave that screams for justice. I'm

shackled there, hoping to plane the land square. I'm a slave of hope—remembering a covenant cut from blood of painful price and scarred

beauty. It's lower and darker than this, and its story is uglier for the just unjustly justified. When everything around me says "no" in striking black-

and-white, a death-defying ray of yellow hope pierces the night to say,
"Yes, yes, yes."

ROAD MAP TO JOY

The pandemic was a dark time globally. I felt unprepared, but my husband and I cried out to God for healing and help every day. We felt impotent to change or help. We remembered the dying and the grieving and longed for it to end. We didn't know who to believe or what to do. In time it subsided, but nobody escaped without a scar. Why did God allow it? I don't have the answer. I know that when I prayed, I could see hope far off, shimmering in the dark and sadness. During this time, our pathways to joy were weapons of life that helped us bear up—not losing our sense of humor, nature walks, serious prayer, worship and praise, and lots of good food and movies. I pray we never have this again, but there are situations in life when you feel stuck and can't move or change a thing. There is always a pathway to joy, a lifeline to hope if you choose it.

Scripture
"Rejoice always, pray continually, give thanks in all circumstances; for this is God's will for you in Christ Jesus" (1 Thess. 5:16–18).

Prayer
Dear Lord, strengthen my faith and calm my heart when my world has turned to darkness without any understanding or explanation. Help me learn to make a sacrifice of praise when it seems to be the last thing on earth that I should do. I know there is power in my offering.

Activation
There is a difference in thanking God for affliction and thanking Him amid the heartache. Your prayers of gratefulness do not condone the evil and pain around you. They pierce through it to make God the King over all. He alone is worthy no matter what is happening in your world. He alone is worthy even if your circumstances never change in this lifetime.

Further Study
Romans 13:12–13, 1 Peter 1:13, and Ephesians 6:11

Recommended Reading
One Thousand Gifts: A Dare to Live Fully Right Where You Are by Ann Voskamp

> *Pride gets no pleasure out of having something, only out of having more of it than the next man.*
>
> —C. S. LEWIS

17

Confessions of a Desperate Heart

I am always moved and convicted when I read the sayings of the Desert Fathers. The monastical, earthly saints move my spiritual life to greater heights. They lived in desert caves, away from worldly wiles, to get to know their Creator and Beloved Savior in the suffering of His death and joy of His resurrection. Their sacrifices allowed them to experience redemptive life more fully.

These hermits, whose teaching may seem extreme in our world, purposely deprived themselves of comfort so they could understand the sufferings of Jesus, gain a hold over human passions, and worship God in the purest light. Today the Church teaches grace. The kind of grace that declares such self-deprivation and suffering unnecessary and wasted—a symptom of not fully realizing the complete work of the cross. I am not willing to discard the gems left behind by these stalwart men simply because of the roughness of the coffers that protect them.

They have so much to teach me! Honestly, I think I need a good dose of self-denial to find peace in God's quiet center for the journey ahead. The fruit of their extremity is daily nourishment for me. It is refreshing to meditate on the words they carved out of the destitution of hot desert sands and rock-hard, cold caves of secluded prayer, watching, fasting, and humility.

> The man who follows Christ in solitary mourning is greater than he who praises Christ amid the congregation of men.[2]

At first this statement almost seems erroneous. What could be greater than praising God in the sanctuary with other believers? Indeed, He is worthy. Scripture has much to say about not neglecting gathering, for it strengthens our faith, encourages unity, and gives back to God what is due Him.

Today, the church has little to say about the importance of mourning. However, this Desert Father has the nerve to state that mourning is greater than praise in the congregation! I know it does not carry the weight of biblical truth. But some who sought God more profoundly than I found truth in it, which demands that I must pause and meditate on the notion.

The leading man of the Reformation, Martin Luther is often paraphrased, "Mourning is a rare herb."[3] It is something we don't see very often—a rare commodity. From Matthew 5, consider, "Blessed are the poor in spirit," and, "Blessed are those who mourn" (vv. 3–4).

How often do you find a person truly "poor in spirit" and "mournful?" These ideas are not about poverty or bereavement. They speak of humility and grief over sin and the condition of humankind without God—the ability to hate your sin and keep hating it. To live in the reality that there is no good thing in me without His grace—to recognize self-sufficiency, self-promotion, self-will, self-righteousness, self-reliance, self, self, self, is worldly thinking. I mourn deeply over the things that raise themselves against the knowledge of God in my life.

I was recently very moved by these examples of godly men: John Bradford, one of the four pillars of the Reformation, was burned at the stake in 1555 for his Protestant faith. Filled with humility, he is famously known to have said while viewing a thief being led to the gallows, "There, but for the grace of God, go I."[4] This phrase has since been firmly established among English-speaking people. He refused the opportunity to deny Christ and died asking forgiveness for the people of England who betrayed him. It is written that scarcely a day passed that he did not weep for his sins.

Our brand of Christianity weeps over sin, maybe once—at the time of salvation. Then we are done with that, washed our hands of that. We want the abundant life!

A great missionary to the American Indians in the 1500s, David Brainerd once walked into the forest alone to contemplate his sins. He felt his own depravity so profoundly that he thought the ground would open and swallow him into hell. So deep was his sin that when he returned to camp, he hid his face for fear those around would know how full of pride and unrighteousness he really was.

Once, Paul murdered Christians. I am sure that rattled his cage until the day he passed into glory. And Jesus ... Man of Sorrows. His own rejected Him. Nothing hurts worse. He took time to mourn and fully embrace the rejection of His Father when He bore our sins.

I have been in a time of great weakness in my life. I feel spent after fifty-plus years of service. As I seek restoration and new strength to press on with the journey, my initial reaction is to pursue pleasure and enjoyment. This is the world's understanding of recreation. But I know deep inside that what is really needed here is a good dose of mourning and humility.

I enter a roomful of people with the desire to fill every inch of it with myself. I take the opportunity to talk about myself and how God is using me, how I am reaching out to others, and how I am making a difference—how important I am to His plan and what I have done. My funny stories. My influence. My gift of sacrifice. My connections. The favor God is showing me.

How little I listen. How unwilling I am to move off center stage and let the conversation be about others. How unwilling I am to let others shine. To be poor in spirit. To mourn.

Oh, I am willing to grieve when my health is broken, or my finances are threatened, or when I am not able to climb the ladder of success like my neighbor. Suddenly, it is not so hard. But can I mourn my sinful state when life is good? Can I even see myself without God's favor when things are going well?

I have come to end of my own strength. I have gutted it up for most of my journey.

I must let go and let God do a deeper work.

All my service and work amount to nothing. I am in desperate need.

I remember the old hymn "Come Thou Fount of Every Blessing" by Robert Robinson. The words that are so poignant, they inspire me:

> Prone to wander, Lord, I feel it, prone to leave the God
> I love…bind my wandering heart to Thee.[5]

After so many years of living the high life of grace and forgiveness, service and congregational life, I am *still* prone to wander.

Tears fill my eyes. I close my eyes for the awful glimpse of me. I repent and embrace silence.

ROAD MAP TO JOY

I must agree with the Desert Father. The joy of congregational worship is precious, but there is a place for mourning. There is a place for holy laughter and unconventional behavior in times of revival, but there must be a place for mourning and embracing humility.

And I am asking myself today, "Am I willing to mourn?"

Confession: I just can't go on unless I am.

Scripture
"Blessed are they that mourn, for they shall be comforted" (Matt. 5:4).

Prayer
Dear Lord, I receive Your comfort for my sins and the ways that my actions have fallen short. Help me keep an attitude of mourning and humility all my life. Help me balance this truth with the great joy that comes from dipping deeply into the wells of salvation's freedom.

Activation
It is a precious promise to know that God comforts those who mourn, but this verse in Matthew refers not to sorrow but rather to grief over our failings. This mourning brings us to repentance. Ask the Lord to help you discern the two kinds of mourning and note if they are both active in your life. This has been a lifetime process for me, whose ending brings buckets of joy.

Further Study
Revelation 21:4, 2 Corinthians 7:9–10, and Isaiah 61:2–3

Recommended Reading
The Problem of Pain by C. S. Lewis, and *Respectable Sins: Confronting the Sins We Tolerate* by Jerry Bridges

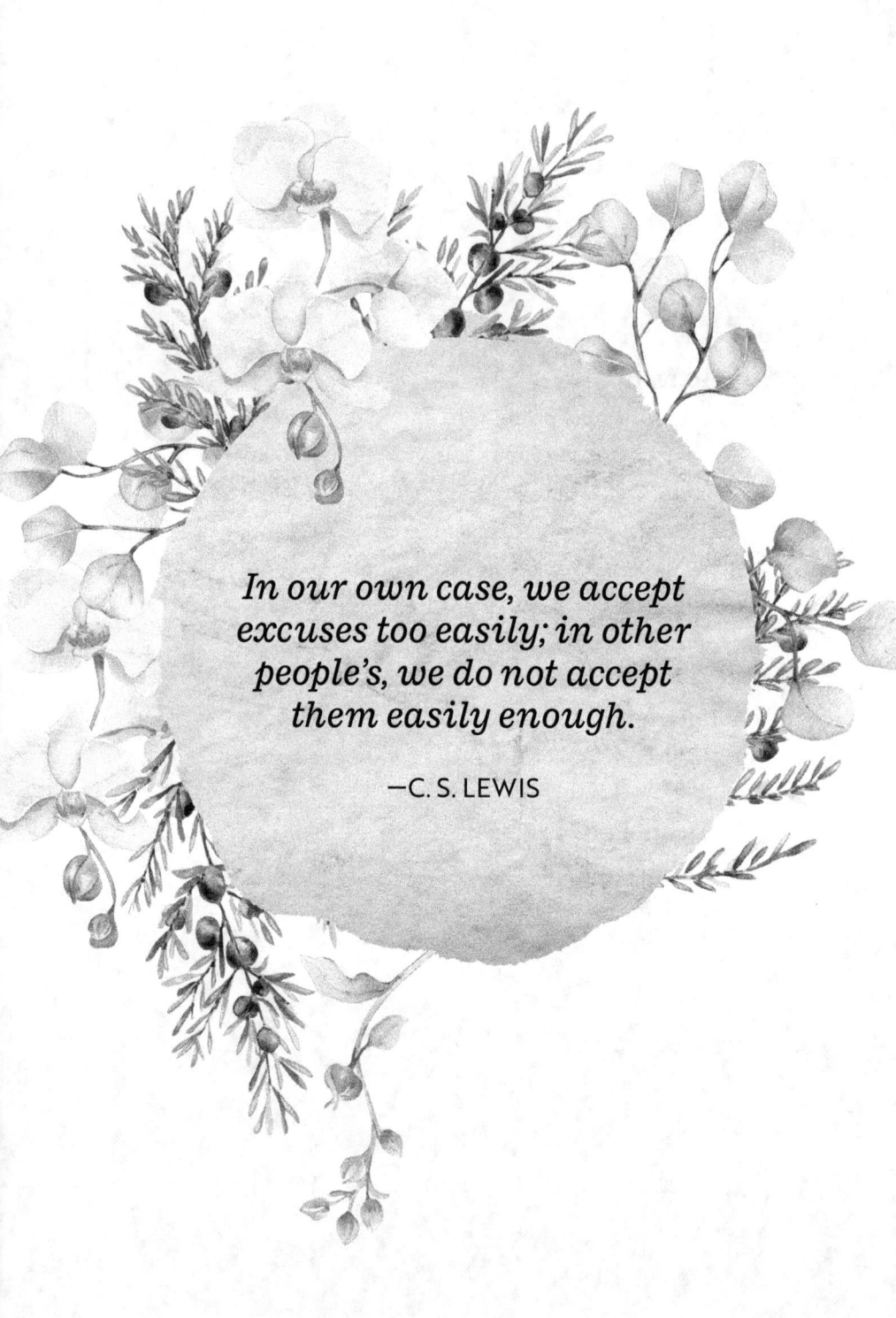

18

The Riverbanks of Tomorrow

I'm passing by car the miles of Ireland and Scotland, and a million dewy green grass blades and pink sea flowers blur with speed. Strangely, the

narrow roads, lined with old stony fences, magnify as we pass. I'm lost in
the thoughts of tomorrow's transition, contemplating if the banks of the

river, that held yesterday's personal dreams, will widen or narrow in the world that stretches beyond the change for which I prepare.

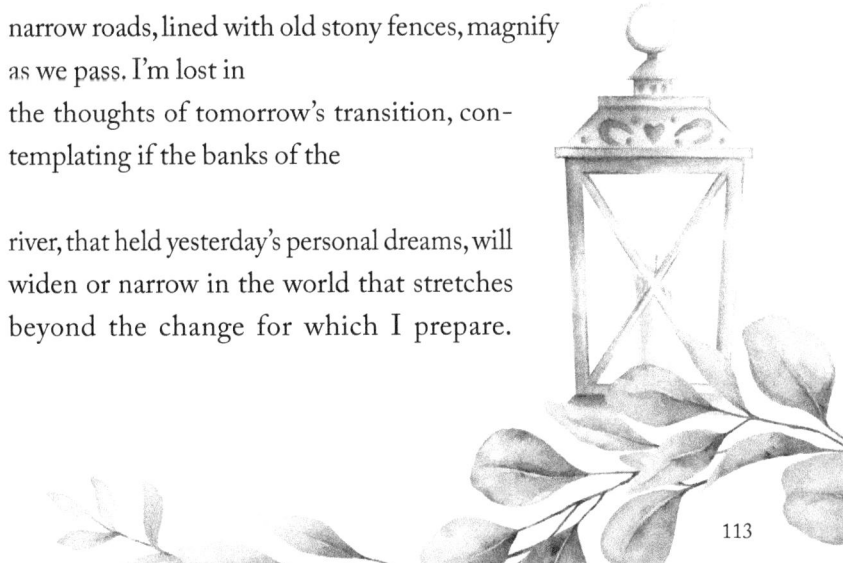

At the same time, I'm reading a book on *acedia*, an old-world word for *apathy*. At its archaic root, it means self-neglect. As one Desert Father wisely

observed, acedia is possibly the root of all human depravity. The cure for self-neglect is the tender loving care and embrace of the

minute details of the life for which one becomes a steward— even the tiny bits that are so boring that they are beneath time, energy, and attention. I'm

thinking about my house at home, full of messy drawers and closets, and a sigh of utter boredom escapes my mouth. The image of beloved Brother

Andrew of French monastic renown, who found the joy of life and strength
of God in the gritty, grubby, boring mundane of service, passes through my

mind. Rising no higher than a servant in this life, he wears a heavenly crown now. Here I am in ancient Scotland now soaking in the Highlands,

wild spring flowers and taking to heart the old-trodden paths of kings and conquerors. I'm inhaling the beauty and pressing my ear to the heart of

Jesus, straining to hear about my tomorrows, but this thought begs for my attention. I don't know how the river will bend in the future, but I'm returning home determined to clean—tenderly and lovingly, my cabinets, closets, and drawers, to put them in right order. This is

the self-neglect to which I am entangled, because I have been preparing and waiting for a Christian calling or duty, more profound.

ROAD MAP TO JOY

Writer and poet Kathleen Norris has had a profound influence on my life. Every book and word opened clear channels of thinking in my head and pathways of action in my heart. I read her book, *Acedia and Me: A Marriage, Monks, and a Writer's Life*[6], while traveling with my daughter and husband through the Highlands of Scotland. I wrote this poem as we passed the miles and hours in such ethereal splendor, such as I had never witnessed. During the journey I endeavored to bring the opposite message of these two extremes into one insightful spiritual application. I knew God was underscoring a useful life tool.

Norris poignantly explains that acedia is physical and spiritual apathy that inhibits our ability to live joyfully and dutifully in God's presence and promises. Her message shook me awake. I still glean from her thoughts and actions on how she overcame.

Scripture
"Above all else, guard your heart, for everything you do flows from it. Keep your mouth free of perversity; keep corrupt talk far from your lips. Let your eyes look straight ahead; fix your gaze directly before you. Give careful

thought to the paths for your feet and be steadfast in all your ways. Do not turn to the right or the left; keep your foot from evil" (Prov. 4:23–27).

Prayer
Dear Lord, may the action of service awaken my enthusiasm and joy for Your calling upon my life.

Activation
The first step to dealing successfully with acedia is to recognize and name it in your life, without shame. Apathy, boredom, frustration, and even laziness strike every human at some juncture. The remedy can be swift and is found by giving of yourself in service of others. It is the pathway to joy. Volunteer in the community or church and in a new way—one that takes you out of your comfort zone. This humble act of service will jolt life's acedia spaces into joyful and rewarding acts of kindness. Or you can spring-clean your house as I did. It woke me up to much more than housework!

Further Study
Romans 16:20, 2 Timothy 4:22, and 2 Corinthians 13:14

The sons of light, along with creation, writhe together awaiting the glorious kiss of new life unfurled—green leaf, fragrant bloom, and sweet fruit—hiding under winter's beautiful, barren branches, so severe, so filigreed.

Upon This Tree

Courage is not simply one of the virtues, but the form of every virtue at the testing point.
—C. S. Lewis

>　　Dead upon this tree,
>　　　I am like You, unresponsive
> To the lower parts of me—
> That crooked bend of the
> Self-slathered dark of foolish pride.
> Risen to live from the roots,
> I am like You. Quickened with
> Life that crushed the gates of hell.
> Dressed in glories of white, dipped in
> Blood. High melodies of light I sing.
> The leaves of this tree are unseen, secure

And flourishing by the Crystal River. They are
Healing hearts, building bridges, salving
Wounds, succoring the savage, binding bruises,
Stripping the thorny rose, now fragrant of dew.

ROAD MAP TO JOY

I love this quote often attributed to C. S. Lewis: "When the whole world is running toward a cliff, he who is running in the opposite directions appears to have lost his mind." I wrote this poem with the same thought in mind—the whole world seems mad, running toward a cliff. Yet the world calls me mad as I ignore that collective groupthink of the day and run with all my might toward the cross of Christ. There I find a shelter filled with the wisdom and power it takes to battle life's wars. The cross is my only hope, salvation, and joy.

Scripture
"For the message of the cross is foolishness to those who are perishing, but to us who are being saved it is the power of God" (1 Cor. 1:18).

Prayer
Dear Lord, help me embrace the humility of the cross and cling to its benefits. Reveal them to me as I bury my life in its shadow.

Activation
Take time to meditate on the foolishness of the cross and the sweet benefits of its glory and triumph. Journal your thoughts for future encouragement. Let pools of joy surround the meditation.

Further Study
Romans 1:16, 2 Corinthians 2:14, and 1 Corinthians 2:2

Recommended Reading
Our Savior's Cries from the Cross by Charles Spurgeon, and *Fifty Reasons Why Jesus Came to Die* by John Piper

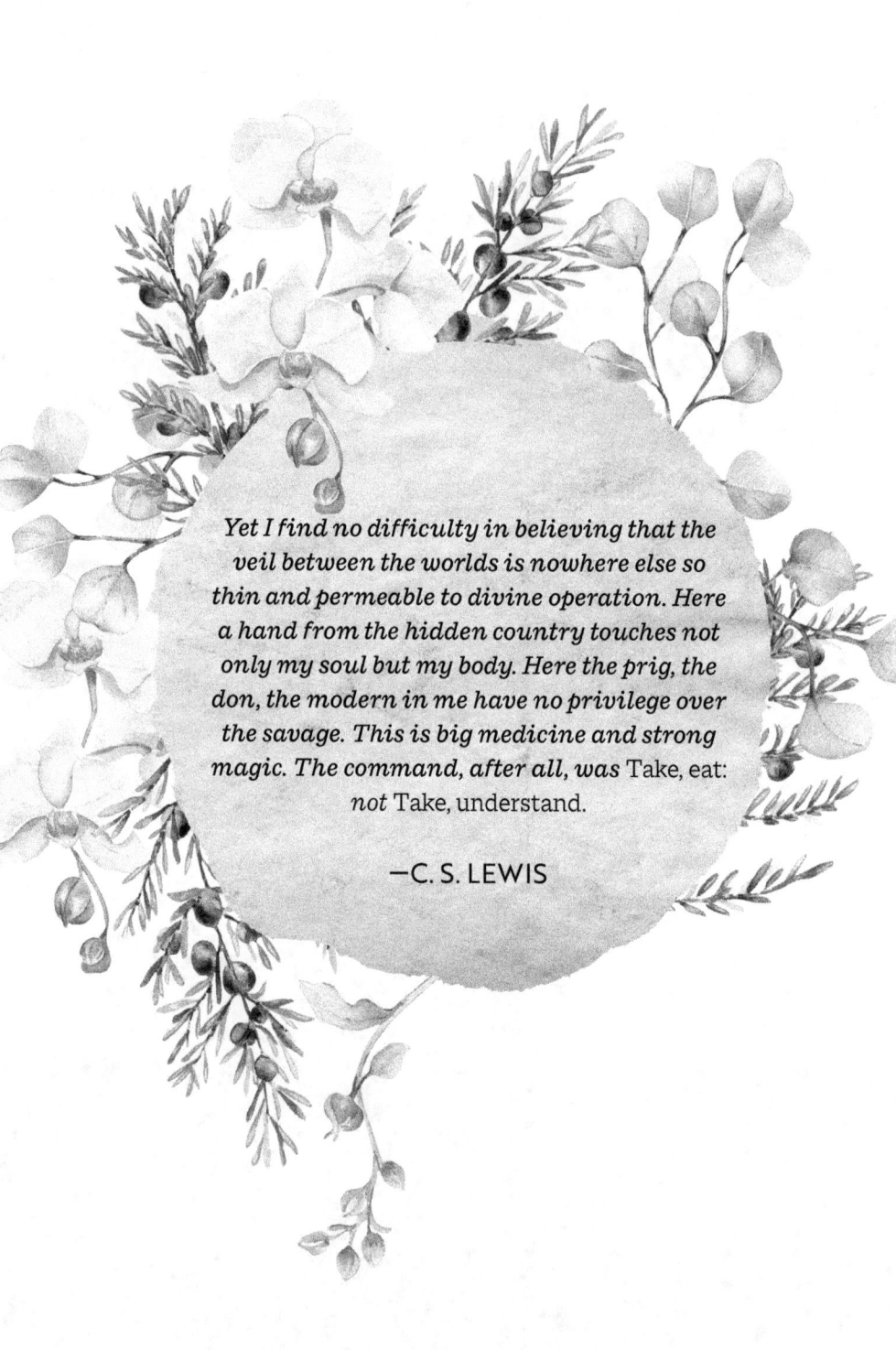

Yet I find no difficulty in believing that the veil between the worlds is nowhere else so thin and permeable to divine operation. Here a hand from the hidden country touches not only my soul but my body. Here the prig, the don, the modern in me have no privilege over the savage. This is big medicine and strong magic. The command, after all, was Take, eat: *not* Take, understand.

—C. S. LEWIS

20

Please Pass the Bread

I love bread too much! That is why it is on the top of the list when I need to fast. A few months ago I went without bread for a few weeks. Feeling deprived, I started dreaming about large sourdough loaves—freshly baked and slathered with butter. Somebody help me!

The good news is that the abstinence brought a spiritual breakthrough. The crack of light illuminating a current problem came straight from heaven, offering me new direction and fresh hope. It also reminded me of my desperate need for heavenly bread and not just hot, buttered sourdough.

The Hebrew word for *bread* is *lechem* (לחם). It derives from the same root as the word for *war*—*milchamah* (מִלְחָמָה). In Hebrew it is very significant when different words share common roots. You are probably asking the same question I did, "What kind of language and culture relates bread with war?" And to complicate things, a third meaning derives from the pure root: *lacham* (לָחַם), "to be joined together." These disparate meanings are born out of the same letter combination past tense root: "he battled," "he ate bread," and "he joined together."

Ludwig Koehler explained that the third root may have reflected the action of being "closely packed together" like in times of war.[8] Before high-tech combat, actual hand-to-hand fighting occurred in tight places. Soldiers stood side-by-side with their comrades and battled face-to-face with their enemies. Also, Koehler suggests that bread is a scarce and nutritious commodity during war. You must have it to continue fighting. Bread and war go hand in hand.

Bread is found in many places in the Bible. When Adam sinned and was banned from the garden of Eden, *be-ze'at apekha tokhal lechem*…"You will eat lechem by the sweat of your brow." Here it means not just bread but food.

The Hebrew Sabbath blessing, "who brings lechem from the earth," also has a dual meaning of bread and food. After the Sabbath prayer, bread is tasted around the table before the meal is eaten.

In Jewish thought, the Torah, or the first five books of the Old Testament, is tasty and nourishing like bread—it should be ingested in the soul and spirit with the same kind of enjoyment and hunger.

I love the story in the book of Ezra when the prophet began to read from the book of the Law of Moses to the people. They stood and listened, with focused attention, from morning until noon. That living bread caused them to repent of their sins and the sins of their parents. They had gained spiritual eyes to recognize the importance of keeping God's covenant.

It's incredible how the people of Israel endured standing "for hours" because they were spiritually starved. Undernourishment in the spirit of man can cause him—or her—to forget physical hunger and discomfort at times because the need for spiritual filling is so innate, so deep, so desperate.

To Christians and Messianic believers, the word *lechem* is powerful. Yeshua—Jesus—was born in Bethlehem, or *beit lechem* (לֶחֶם בֵּית) in Hebrew, meaning "house of bread." This is precious because Jesus is called the "Bread of Life."

Today, I enjoyed my crust of freshly baked bread. It satisfied my body and soul somehow. But I just can't exist without my spiritual bread, God's Holy Word. That, excuse the expression, just takes the cake. It's the heavenly manna that rocks my world, makes me strong in heart, and feel alive!

I think I better get this house picked up today, lest I be accused of eating the "bread of idleness," something a Proverbs 31 woman refuses to do.

ROAD MAP TO JOY

Scripture
"Then Jesus declared, 'I am the bread of life. Whoever comes to me will never go hungry, and whoever believes in me will never be thirsty'" (John 6:35).

Prayer
Dear Lord, help me love Your Word more than the greatest pleasures in this life. Give me a deeper revelation—show me how to apply it daily. Open my eyes to see hidden treasures and mysteries.

Activation
The breaking of bread is both common and mystical. It is daily and yet has the power to make strangers friends and create strong bonds in families through sharing. Meditate on the Hebraic meanings of bread and ask the Lord to show you how they may bring richer meaning to your life as you share around the table. Also, when you take the time to read God's Word each day, consider the nourishment you receive in your spirit as you partake.

Regard it as necessary and not superfluous to your life. Jesus is our daily bread.

There are many ways to whet your spiritual appetite for the nourishment, revelation, and application of the Bible. Here are three that have worked for me.
Join a serious Bible Study group (online and live) such as Bible Study Fellowship.

Inquire in your local church for Bible study groups. Search online for Bible study tools to enhance your personal study.

Further Study
John 6:47–51, Leviticus 22:6–7, and Acts 2:42

Recommended Reading
Eat This Book: A Conversation in the Art of Spiritual Reading by Eugene H. Peterson, and *A Meal with Jesus: Discovering Grace, Community, and Mission Around the Table* by Tim Chester

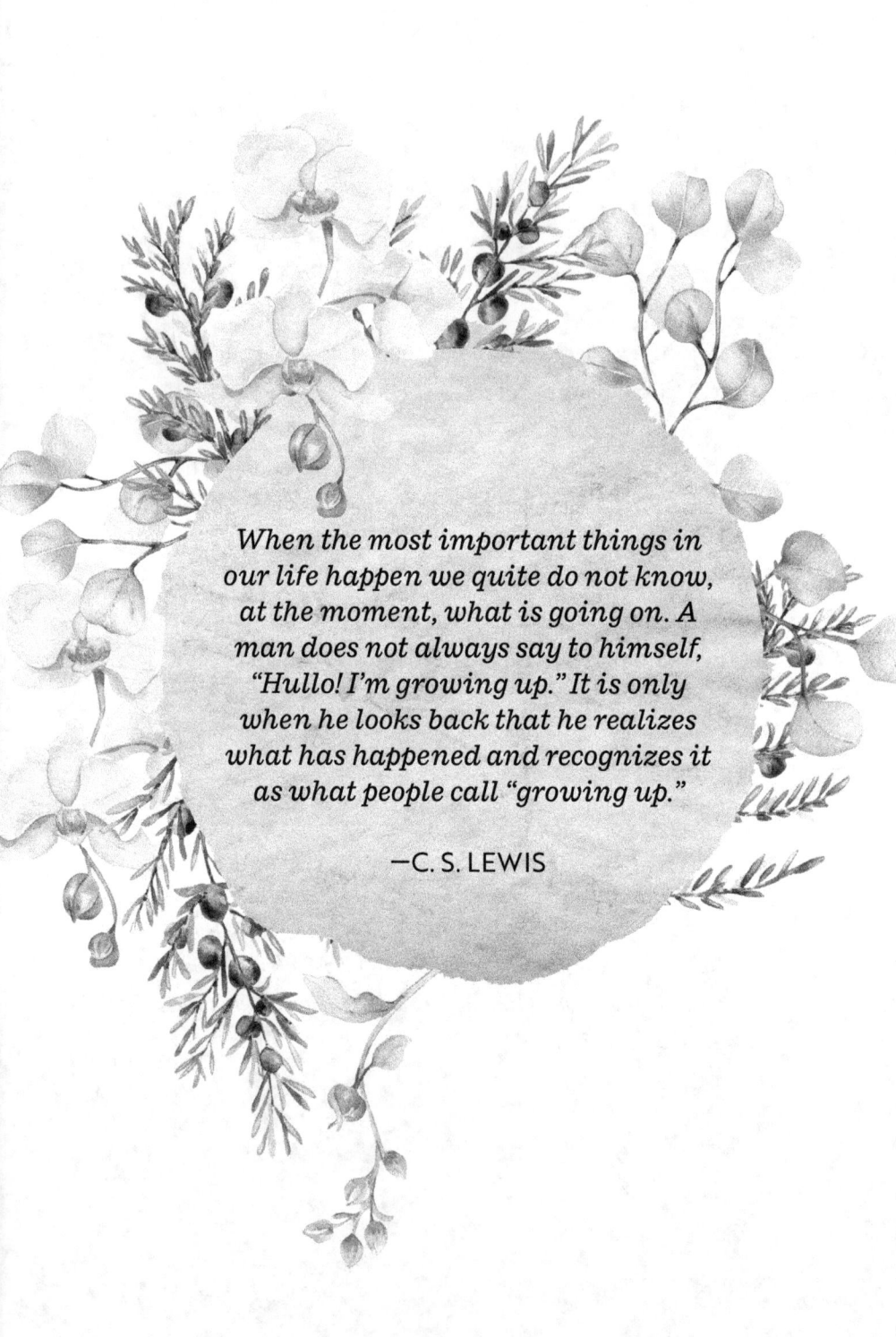

When the most important things in our life happen we quite do not know, at the moment, what is going on. A man does not always say to himself, "Hullo! I'm growing up." It is only when he looks back that he realizes what has happened and recognizes it as what people call "growing up."

—C. S. LEWIS

21

Shades of Violet

When I was in seventh grade, a new girl named Maggie checked into our homeroom class. She shone like a beacon in a dark sky with her curly, shiny, raven hair, beaming brown eyes, and confident smile. To this day I remember those magenta suede go-go boots she glamorously paraded, giving her a decided flare and edge above her peers. That beautiful, blossoming young teenager oozed coolness.

Purple, violet, plum, magenta, amethyst, orchid, wine, or pomegranate—I could not (cannot) resist these shades. They still are my love language of color. My eyes narrowed and grew green with envy over those gorgeous, soft, magenta leather boots, but deep down, I knew only Maggie could wear them with confidence. In the end I admired the new girl in school more than I envied her.

Later, Maggie left school suddenly—we heard her father beat her. I remember thinking about her purple-bruised heart that no one saw when she walked into our class the first day.

Not a flamboyant extrovert like Maggie, I happily sat in the safety of a back corner in our classroom, but I wore purple inside. No one saw the indigo shades in me as I ached because of Maggie's trauma.

Years later words of deepest plum rolled out of me in scarlet ribbons and brought tears, healing streams of perspective, and clarity to the memory of a twelve-year-old girl who awoke suddenly from childhood's blissful innocence to the jolting reality of a violent, violet bruised world.

ROAD MAP TO JOY

Childhood awakenings, drawn from trauma or joy, become the foundations of adulthood. This experience in my early life highlighted that the world has unimaginable pain and suffering, and some around me may be hurting without expression or help. Empathy awoke in me that day as I grew ashamed of my jealousy toward Maggie. I carry this lesson with me always as I connect in friendships, which is what prompted me to write this poem. What brings me joy is that, as an adult, I know God heals the wounds of the hurting, and the deepest, darkest traumas or injustices can be healed with the right tools. I pray Maggie found restoration.

Scriptures
"He heals the brokenhearted and binds up their wounds" (Ps. 147:3).

"When I was a child, I talked like a child, I thought like a child, I reasoned like a child. When I became a man, I put the ways of childhood behind me" (1 Cor. 13:11).

Prayer
Dear Lord, may Your love and compassion be a shield and a balm against childhood or adult trauma or abuse I have suffered.

Activation
In the suffering, especially of childhood trauma, there is often shameful silence and secrecy, and in that reserved reticence, there is immeasurable pain. The first step to breaking the stillness is to begin dialoguing with a cherished friend, a pastor, or a professional counselor. You may find a measure of immediate healing—that will grow wide and deep—just by expressing and releasing the pressure of what has been hidden in darkness. Keep pouring out your words of pain—every sentence can help bring emotional health and newfound pools of joy to your liberation.

Further Study
Psalm 61:1–7, Psalm 34:18, 1 Corinthians 14:20, and Ecclesiastes 11:10

Recommended Reading
Try Softer: A Fresh Approach to Move Us Out of Anxiety, Stress, and Survival Mode—and into a Life of Connection and Joy by Aundi Kolber

> My argument against God was that the universe seemed so cruel and unjust. But how had I got this idea of just and unjust? A man does not call a line crooked unless he has some idea of a straight line. What was I comparing this universe with when I called it unjust?
>
> —C. S. LEWIS

22

Underscoring Justice

It was the best of times, it was the worst of times, it was the age of wisdom, it was the age of foolishness, it was the epoch of belief, it was the epoch of incredulity, it was the season of Light, it was the season of Darkness, it was the spring of hope, it was the winter of despair.[7]

In the opening of the book *A Tale of Two Cities*, Charles Dickens wrote these poignant words in 1859, and they sound like a current newspaper article.

In our wild and random cancel-culture world, justice is of prime importance. Seething protestors march and sometimes loot, burn, and destroy. Social media has become a raging mob demanding personal and group rights. Our social stories of injustice are on visual repeat which often morphs into a frenzy—until someone is harmed or killed. Then we are in shock and again demanding swift and harsh justice.

These actions are about evening the score.

Every soul, at one time or another, feels as if they have gotten a raw deal in life. It comes with being human. God cares about justice; it is a key issue for Him. In heaven His throne room is called Justice.

> Righteousness and justice are the foundation of your throne; love and faithfulness go before you.
> —Psalm 89:14

One of the Bible's main themes is justice. To act in justice means doing what is fair and morally right. If a person is just in lifestyle and choices, they are circumspect in their actions toward others. Simply, they choose to do what is right even at personal cost.

According to the *American Tract Society Bible Dictionary*, God's unswerving justice is described as "the essential and infinite attribute which makes his nature and his ways the perfect embodiment of equity and constitutes him the model and the guardian of equity throughout the universe."[8]

I love that, "the guardian of equity."

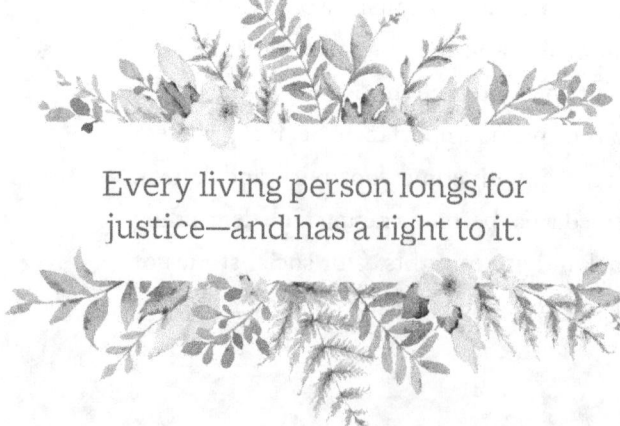

Every living person longs for justice—and has a right to it.

> Learn to do good; seek justice, correct oppression, bring justice to the fatherless, plead the widows' cause.
> —Isaiah 1:17, ESV

> Thus says the LORD: Do justice and righteousness, and deliver from the hand of the oppressor him who has been robbed. And do no wrong or violence to the resident, alien, the fatherless, and the widow, nor shed innocent blood in this place.
> —Jeremiah 22:3, ESV

> The righteous care about justice for the poor, but the wicked have no such concern.
> —Proverbs 29:7

> Evil men do not understand justice, but those who seek the LORD understand it completely.
> —Proverbs 28:5, ESV

One of the darkest times in the history of the world, the Holocaust, brought forth the gravest injustice. In tandem with this event, a horrific terrorist attack occurred on October 7, 2023, when Hamas brutally massacred over one thousand Israeli Jews in their homeland.

During and after these unconscionable crimes against humanity, both Jew and gentile cried out, "Where was God?"

They are still asking, "Where is God?"

I think the viewpoint of Rabbi Jonathan Sacks is worth noting:

> The Holocaust represented perhaps the greatest failure humanity has ever known. It featured the combination of technical brilliance and bureaucratic efficiency but

dedicated to the most evil of all purposes. This really is the greatest failure of humanity that I can think of.[9]

Other rabbis and religious leaders have echoed this inquiry—not, "Where was God?" but, "Where was humanity during the Holocaust?"

Scripture is clear that God has given us commandments and instructions to execute justice in this world. We have limited reach, but we have reach! We are to care for the marginalized, the poor, the widow, the hurting, the weak. Often, we close our eyes to all of this, or we ignore the injustice right before our faces. Somehow we let it slip—thinking someone else will do it or that it's not really that bad. I have been silent myself sometimes. I am ashamed of this. We are all responsible for speaking up for justice and against injustice. It starts in our own families, homes, and neighborhoods as we teach our children what proper justice is. It is our responsibility to be just to one another and to speak up for the justice of others.

Ultimately, God is in control of justice and vengeance. That is why He admonishes us two things: not to stop asking for justice, to keep crying out for it even day and night. He also says that He will bring the full weight of justice along with vengeance to His enemies. He says that we must wait for that justice.

In the meantime, though, there are things we can do on this earth to bring justice, such as speaking up for, giving to, or befriending the marginalized and weak. We must work to understand their plight in this world.

The world is unfair and unjust, but God has given us the power to bring a measure of justice. We need to do all that we can.

ROAD MAP TO JOY

Scriptures
"Justice never makes sense to men devoted to darkness, but those tenderly devoted to the Lord can understand justice perfectly" (Prov. 28:5, TPT).

"And the Lord said, 'Listen to what the unjust judge says. And will not God bring about justice for his chosen ones, who cry out to him day and night? Will he keep putting them off? I tell you; he will see that they get justice, and quickly. However, when the Son of Man comes, will he find faith on the earth?'" (Luke 18:6–8).

Prayer
I thank You, Lord, for caring about justice. Your Word instructs us to cry out for justice and wait for Your way to bring things to light and punish evil.

Activation
The world is buzzing with social issues and righting wrongs in society. Become aware of cases or events of injustice in the world, and learn to speak out against such. First, cry out for justice in prayer. God has promised to hear and answer. Second, show up for the marginalized and forgotten of the earth. Learn their needs and educate others. Be willing to meet what needs you can on your own. Standing against evil in a very dark world brings a joyful reward and often a joyful end.

Further Study
2 Peter 3:8–9, Hebrews 10:23–26, and Matthew 24:9–13

Recommended Reading
Morality: Restoring the Common Good in Divided Times by Jonathan Sacks

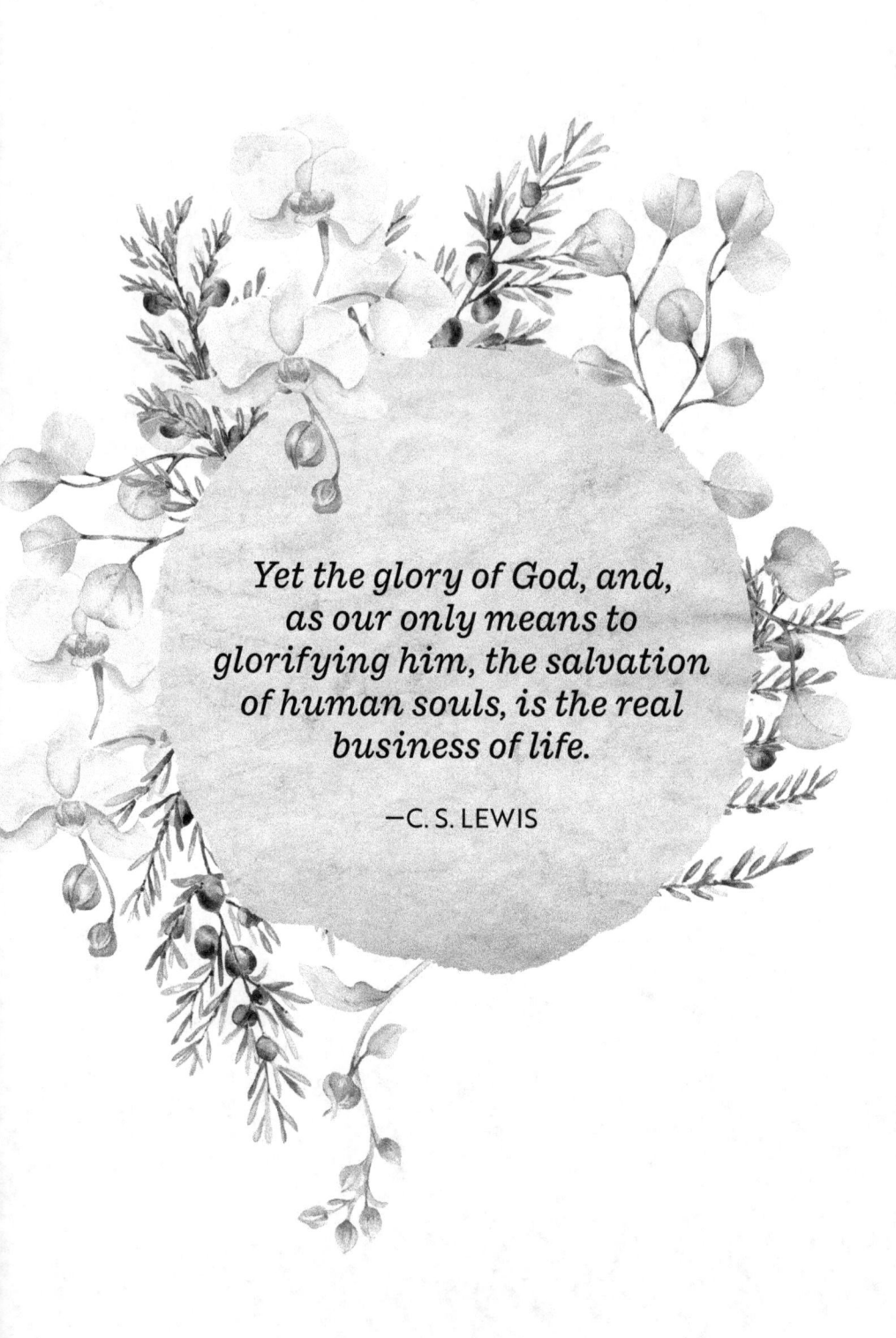

Yet the glory of God, and, as our only means to glorifying him, the salvation of human souls, is the real business of life.

—C. S. LEWIS

On an Irish Cliff

I remember a bright-eyed
girl, full of passion and
young hope, who sat on a
church pew at twelve years old
and sang an old hymn,
earnestly with holy hush
and sincere heart,

"Let the lower lights
keep burning, send the beam
across the way. Some poor
struggling, fearing seaman,
you may rescue, you may save."

Drops of grace rained down
on me in that sanctuary, and my

heart paused with the world in
rapture and sobriety as I
responded to the call to shine
for Jesus, to embrace the need to
go to the nations with the
good news.

And here I stand in Ireland
decades later gazing upon a
lighthouse from a moss-grown
cliff as the Holy Spirit washes
over me a fresh call
to burn on in the dark,
to burn across the waves.
Some to rescue.
Some to save.

I brush away the tears
remembering the little girl who
heard the call long ago.
I wonder where she is.

The Irish wind blows over me
and I taste salt on my lips. Oh,
that little girl is still here.
She's still here,
burning,
still willing to go.

ROAD MAP TO JOY

The call to be a light to the nations originated with the people of Israel. By the kindness of God we are included and brought near to the blessings and callings of the commonwealth of Israel (Eph. 2:11–13). As a gentile believer, my sweetest church memories are hearing the call of God to be a missionary.

Missionary is a hated word among Jewish people and some Messianic believers, and for good reason—such atrocities through the centuries have been committed against God's ancient people in the name of the Church or missions.

Perhaps becoming a light in the darkness is more appropriate. When I responded, little did I know it would mean serving the Jewish people around the world. My husband and I have traveled hundreds of thousands of miles and have shared the love of Yeshua with Holocaust survivors, the lost tribes of Africa, Jews in South America, and across Europe and the former Soviet Union. It has been our greatest joy to be a light to Israel and to help them shine as a light to the nations.

Scripture
"It is too small a thing for you to be my servant to restore the tribes of Jacob and bring back those of Israel I have kept. I will also make you a light for the Gentiles, that my salvation may reach to the ends of the earth" (Isa. 49:6).

Prayer
Dear Lord, change my heart so it yearns for the good news of the gospel to be preached in every nation and in every language. Deepen my anguish for those sitting in the darkness of sin and self-sufficiency without the true light of salvation.

Activation
From time to time the passion of your calling must be washed and renewed. Allow the Holy Spirit to remind you of your first calling—dedicate yourself to it with fresh courage and strength. Make plans to go again and shine your light. If you have never taken a short-term or long-term missions trip, take the initiative. It will change your life and bring abundant joy.

Further Study
Acts 13:47, Psalm 98:2–3, and Acts 26:18

If the whole universe has no meaning, we should never have found out that it has no meaning: just as, if there were no light in the universe and therefore no creatures with eyes, we should never know it was dark. Dark would be without meaning.

—C. S. LEWIS

24

Confessions of a Cosmic Outcast

I love the line in the movie *Contact* starring Jodie Foster, when she was traveling through space and beholding wonders and beauty unlike anything on earth: "They shouldn't have sent a scientist to describe this; they should have sent a poet."[10]

Nice compliment from the scientist to the poet! The splendor of space, stars, and galaxies is certainly worthy of the expression of poetry.

As a little girl I sat on the front porch night after night and fell in love with the heavens. My memories are vivid: the cool night air, the inky black sky, and the sparkling stars singing against the velvet dark. I heard their songs. And I sang too, all alone in my girlish meditations, private symphonies of praise to my Maker, who created in glory the planets beyond our world. In my ponderings, I saw the vast majestic universe first; then, I saw the form of God holding it all together. I longed for Him.

On those inspirational nights alone in the starlight, one scripture from the psalms came to me over and over, "Be still, and know I am God" (Ps. 46:10).

The dark sky, the twinkling stars, and the awesomeness of God who made all creation visible and invisible, overwhelmingly vast, limitless, beyond comprehension. Still, the weight of this knowledge did not crush me—I did not feel insignificant. I felt the opposite—God had something important for me to contribute—my life had meaning, purpose, and order just like the universe.

Later in life, I discovered that culture pulled against those childhood feelings. The colloquial intellect and learning of the times taught that man had zero significance in the role and plan of the universe—that there was, in fact, no plan at all.

Immanuel Kant, an eighteenth-century German philosopher, wrote that the vastness of the universe destroys the importance of humankind.[11] Friedrich Nietzsche, the nineteenth-century atheist, said that we are cosmic outcasts.[12] Despite the conflicting opinions in the culture around me, I grew to find great contentment in what a young shepherd boy wrote about the universe:

> When I consider Your heavens, the work of Your fingers, the moon and the stars, which You have ordained, what is man that you are mindful of him, and the son of man that You visit him?
>
> For you have made him a little lower than the angels, and You have crowned him with glory and honor.

You have made him to have dominion over the works
of Your hands; You placed all things under his feet.
—Psalm 8:3–6, NKJV

I believe God created the heavens with extravagance to prove, every day as we enjoy it, that He is capable of extravagant love. He ordained it so we could learn to measure it, study it, and draw closer to Him.

God intends for the vastness of the universe, known and unknown, to compel us to know the designer and artist and His intimate love for mankind.

The educated men of my day had labeled me a "cosmic outcast," but my personal experience and testimony is the opposite.

ROAD MAP TO JOY

My prayer is that the awesome, extravagant God of the universe will draw each person out into the starry nights. I pray one by one each will sit in the silence of His heart, looking up at the stars and discovering they are significant to God's eternal plan—that the despised and rejected Jesus is both the Creator and the Lamb who takes away the sins of the whole world.

Scripture
"Lift up your eyes and look to the heavens: Who created all these? He who brings out the starry host one by one and calls forth each of them by name. Because of his great power and mighty strength, not one of them is missing" (Ps. 40:26).

Prayer
Dear Lord, awaken my heart to know You more intimately when I see the beauty and splendor of the universe You made.

Activation

If you do not believe in Jesus, then pause to ponder this question: Has there ever been a time when you looked at the universe and stars and imagined someone greater? Do you remember that young faith that instilled hope? That deep-down longing for intimacy cannot be fulfilled by humankind alone. Only God fits into that hole. Pray for a childlike revelation of Jesus as the expressed image of the Creator in bodily form. Ask for a sign that will reveal this truth to you and for the grace to receive it. Salvation will bring you depths of joy!

Further Study
1 Corinthians 5:7, Revelation 13:8, and John 1:29

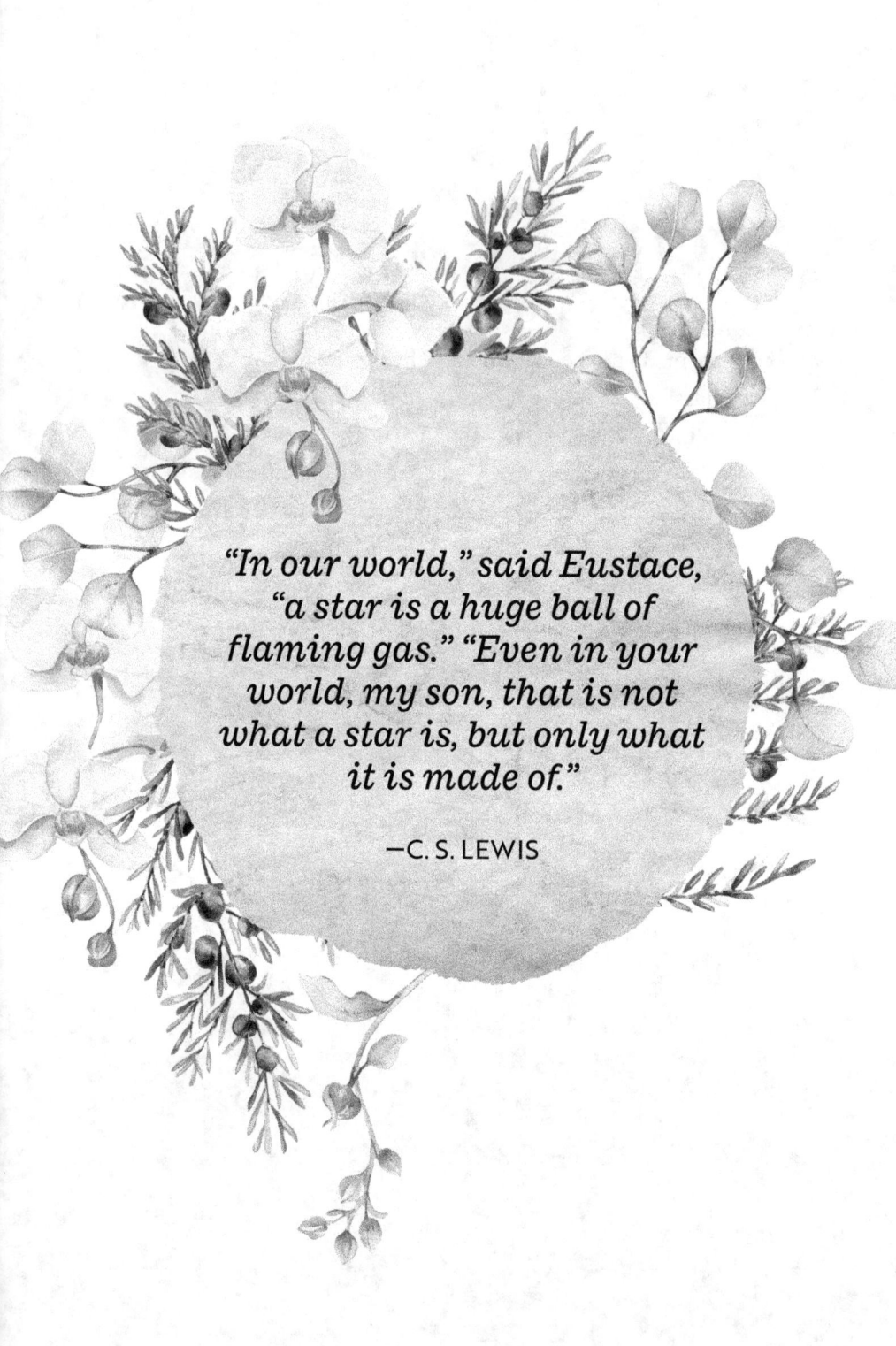

"In our world," said Eustace, "a star is a huge ball of flaming gas." "Even in your world, my son, that is not what a star is, but only what it is made of."

—C. S. LEWIS

25
Leaning on the Stars

Rising from the fog,
Pulled upward by Your
Dazzling wake of light,
Above the cool garden,
Above the wet, morning grass
And weeping willows,
Majestically soaring over ancient oaks
And waving heads of golden grain,
I am anchored in the clouds—
Leaning on the stars that You named.
Falling into Your strong arms of love,
I am captivated for eternity.
When I breathe, I breathe Jesus.

ROAD MAP TO JOY

When I was growing up, I would sit outside on the front porch at night and watch the inky bluish-black sky and the stars. "Be still, and know that I am God," was what the Holy Spirit whispered in my heart. During the 1960s, it was popular not to believe in God. The German philosopher Friedrich Nietzsche's claim that "God is dead"[13] was gaining cultural momentum. I knew this was a lie. I raised my arms and stated that He was alive. It was my childhood resistance against the waves of godless culture assailing the world. And you know what? I still love to stargaze. It brings me great joy. I still proclaim, "God is not dead."

Scripture
"The heavens declare the glory of God; the skies proclaim the work of his hands. Day after day they pour forth speech; night after night they reveal knowledge. They have no speech; they use no words; no sound is heard from them. Yet their voice goes out into all the earth, their words to the end of the world" (Ps. 19:1–4).

Prayer
I thank You, Lord, for Your beautiful creation, especially the night sky, filled with wonders of light that reflect Your glory. Help me pause and peer up, be still and know that You are God.

Activation
Take time and sit outside weekly to stargaze, praising Him for this pleasure. Make it your own kind of resistance against the falsehoods of our culture that assail us, rob our joy, and mock our faith. Stargazing with joy is an act of resistance.

Further Study
Psalm 50:6, Romans 1:19–20, and Genesis 1:14–15

For the Past is frozen and no longer flows, and the Present is all lit up with eternal rays.

—C. S. LEWIS

26

Stability in New Beginnings

I am listening to the early rain, drinking morning coffee, meditating on the open road before me as a new year begins.

The scripture the Lord gave me for this fresh season came white-hot with hope:

And He will be the stability of your times, a wealth of salvation, wisdom, and knowledge; the fear of the Lord is his treasure.
—Isaiah 33:6, NASB

Stability is my word of promise. Tomorrow the number 365 stretches before me, fresh and clean, unknown. Steadiness is such a great promise from a good Father, yet it is a common attribute, so it is easy to diminish its value. It means standing on a solid foundation—the kind that allows me to launch forward into supernatural endurance. It means that the steps beneath me enlarge as I journey, making my pathway solid. It means that chaos has turned to normalcy. This anchor of stability serves as solid hope through shifting transitions that I cannot control.

The Hebrew word for *stability* is *emunah* (אֱמוּנָה), deriving from the word *firmness*. In modern Hebrew it is used daily as the word for *faith*. What a beautiful idea—to equate stability and faith. Faith makes you stable or firm, and stability increases faith or firmness.

That verse goes on to say that Christ is the stability of our times, a wealth of salvation, wisdom, and knowledge.

> As we daily abide in Jesus, seeking Him through worship and daily feasting on the Word, stability anchors us by giving us salvation, wisdom, and knowledge.

These gifts help us navigate uncertainty.

The world emerged from the darkness of COVID-19 bruised—spirit, soul, and body. It's already years later, and the world has had so many shifts that stability hovers on the distant horizon like an elusive dream.

The petals of my youth are quickly falling, yet I am deeply rooted beside ageless rivers of living water. There is change, and there is normalcy. At the turning of a new season, I understand that the flower will fade, but the leaf will not waste away. It is medicine for healing the nations. I will always cling to these truths.

I am stepping into the uncharted pathway of the future with faith and expectancy. I am pressing deeper into the unknown—not with strife or labor but with the same unbending violence that brought a dark kingdom down and triumphed in victory at Calvary.

I am at war, and yet the war has been won. I am sober yet full of joy for what lies ahead. I am willing to change yet rejoicing in what remains the same. I am anchored with a stability that defies human comprehension. I am stepping into the unrevealed without a road map, rather a code of conduct that has been blood-washed and saturated with grace. My steps are unfamiliar, and yet I know God is leading, refining my life as I go, like silver is purified in the heat of battle.

ROAD MAP TO JOY

As I cross into the future, I know that when my life is jolted by unstable people or circumstances, salvation, wisdom, and knowledge are present. My heart is full and overflowing as I try to wrap my head around this beautiful promise. Stability is available to me. When I pray, He answers. Truly we live and operate in an unseen kingdom, enjoying God's steady hand when the world is going topsy-turvy.

Scripture
"For he will never be shaken; the righteous will be remembered forever. He will not fear bad news; his heart is steadfast, trusting in the Lord. His heart is firm, he will not fear" (Ps. 112:6–8).

Prayer
Dear Lord, be the stability of my times. Calm my anxious thoughts and fill my heart with Your peace. Guide me with Your wisdom as I plan daily and beyond.

Activation

As you navigate life changes, it is important to remember that God's peace and wisdom are always available to you. No matter what you are dealing with—health issues, loss of a job, a difficult decision, or the unknowns of the future—God will be with you to guide and protect you. Be familiar with His promises and rehearse them often. Pray frequently, making your requests known to Him. He will give peace, joy, and direction.

Further Study
Philippians 4:6–7, Proverbs 19:23, and Psalm 112:1–3

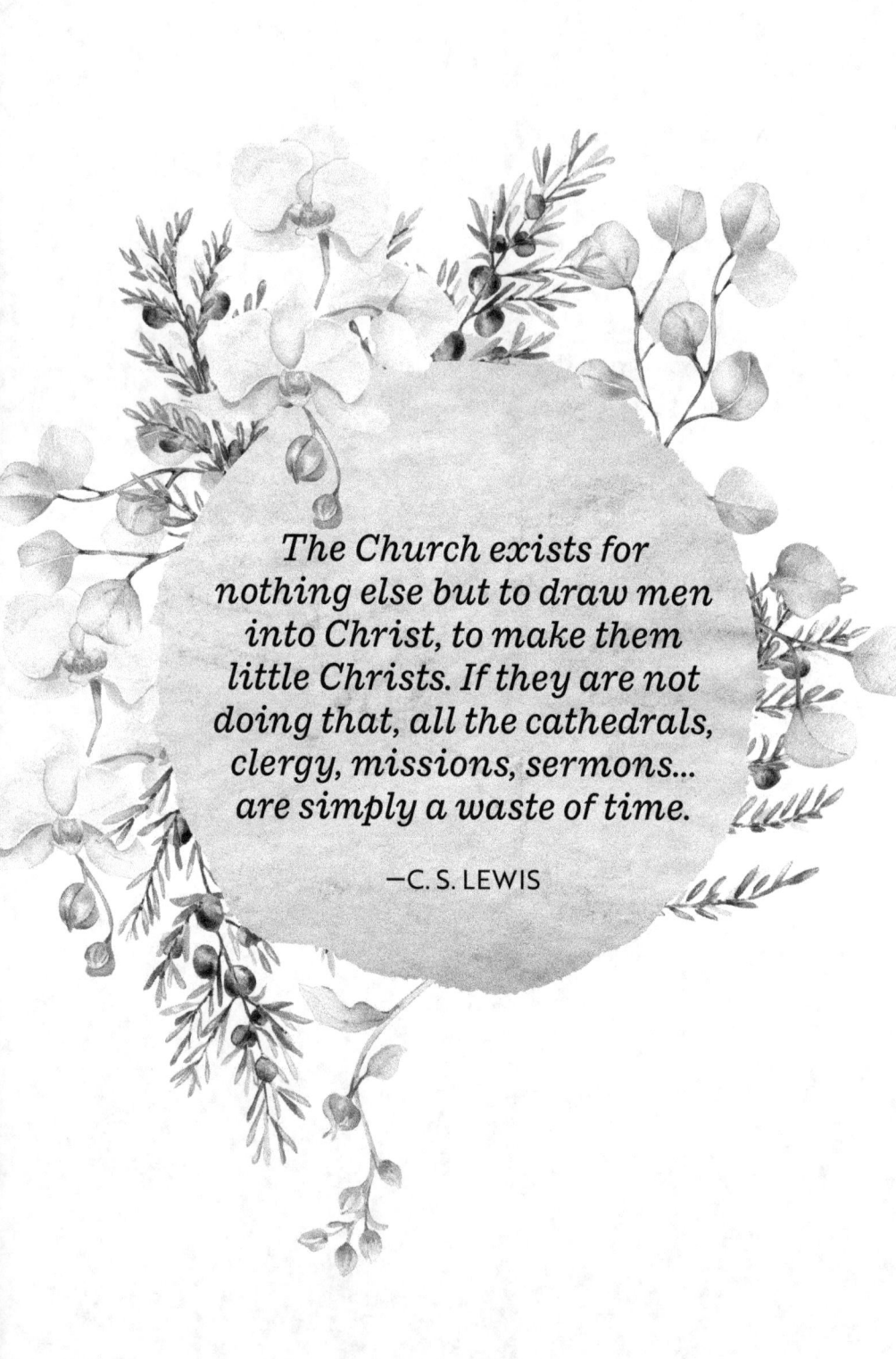

> The Church exists for nothing else but to draw men into Christ, to make them little Christs. If they are not doing that, all the cathedrals, clergy, missions, sermons... are simply a waste of time.
>
> —C. S. LEWIS

27

Soul and Spirit

The searching-truth poet
asks with every word penned,
"Is the soul awake?"
assuming that all revelation
finds epiphany in that
ascendancy. But the
dead man knows that the
spirit must arise to life.
And you recognize that
life teems with life
when the sword of betrayal
pierces the heart, and the
spirit pauses
before retaliation
to consider the source of
pain—to weigh reaction

> considering how you've hurt
> and betrayed others and
> been forgiven.
> No, the soul isn't big enough
> for this,
> but the spirit—awakened
> and trained by resurrection
> power—ever magnifies
> perception through love
> and wisdom by withstanding,
> through grace,
> the rigors of life's assaults.

I wrote this poem during the hardest year of my life as a woman, pastor's wife, missionary, and Christian. Several (I could say many, seventy-five to date!) moral failures among pastors and parachurch leaders had been uncovered nationally—in different places around the states and from varying religious affiliations—had been exposed, with the leaders accused of serious sexual sins. Some of these egregious incidents became international news. After the jolt of pain and loss, the trauma began to hurt, and I began to seek God earnestly to receive more understanding and light—not so much, "Why?" but rather, "Where do we, as the body of Christ, go from here, and what is there to learn?"

I wept for weeks and prayed. Many, both within and outside the Church, began to point long fingers of accusation, demanding God's swift and brutal justice. Others insisted that all could be or had been forgiven, so we must move on to complete the task of pursuing God's kingdom first. In some weird and conflicting way, both camps upheld a strong standard of truth.

Mercy and restoration are available to all who truly repent. God loves and draws both the perpetrator and survivor to Himself with loving cords of compassion. But ultimate healing and redemption require the cooperation all parties, as well as earthly authority and spiritual leadership given charge of the fold. Some sins disqualify leaders. The Church must face this fact with sobriety. Safeguards must be set in place to aid survivors and deal with dangerous leadership. Although forgiven at the cross, they must take the consequences of the world and code of societal morality that we live in according to the offense.

As the quiet voice of the Holy Spirit reminded me of God's perfect mercy and justice, I sat down to write about all that was racing through my heart and head. The conclusion of the poem surprised me. I felt waves of pain and compassion for both the sinner and the sinned against. In the end I had no words of accusation to level and no one to blame—my only cry was, "How have I missed the mark in this?" I too have been forgiven much and need abundant mercy.

ROAD MAP TO JOY

The pathways of mercy and justice are intertwined and then separated, depending on the level of repentance. Mercy is plenteous and available, but the laws of sowing and reaping are hard, unchanging, and required until righteousness is fully satisfied. Thank God for the blood of Jesus, which satisfies every demand of justice and lavishes us with mercy we could never earn. His laws are immutable—but so is His love.

Scripture
"Be kind and compassionate to one another, forgiving each other, just as in Christ God forgave you" (Eph. 4:32).

Prayer
Dear Lord, I realize that no one has suffered more than Jesus on the cross for my sins and failings. Still, I feel the pain of betrayal and loss. Please give me the courage to forgive as I have been forgiven. Heal my wounds and cleanse my heart. Forgive the body of Christ for allowing unaccountability to thrive among leadership. Make us humble and forgiving.

Activation

Many offenses in life are between God and me. I am totally open to expressing my hurt and disappointment in others, and sometimes even in Him, when I can't comprehend the plan or don't have all the puzzle pieces to the situation. This kind of transparency is very healing and stabilizing in life's journey. Occasionally, though, you may need to ask for forgiveness face-to-face or broach a personal problem with a perceived enemy. Ask for wisdom, humility, and grace when this is necessary. Rivers of joy overflow when you follow through with making things as right as you can.

Perhaps church leadership has disappointed you or abused you. There is a place of healing for you at the feet of Jesus. Find trusted people with whom you can confide and seek professional help. Keep focused on Jesus, who endured the cross for the joy set before Him.

Further Study
Mark 11:25, 1 John 1:9, and Luke 6:37

God is not merely good, but goodness; goodness is not merely divine, but God.

—C. S. LEWIS

28

Knowing God's Goodness

A very dear friend lost her twelve-year-old son in a fire several years ago. It was heart-wrenching, and we all mourned with the family. Our community of believers surrounded them with comfort, but the weight of this heartbreaking loss was beyond understanding.

About three months after her son's death, many from our group were in Rome, Italy, for a prayer initiative. One morning we gathered in the hotel for a time of worship and intercession. My dear friend fell on her face sobbing, "I must know God is good to go on." It was a very grievous and poignant moment. Her transparency ran so deep and real—her question was raw and appropriate. I agreed when I heard her sobbing, "Yes, God, show us Your goodness."

The entire prayer coalition fell on their faces, weeping in response. The moment stands out as one of the most holy and significant prayers of my life. I could hear muffled sobs as we humbly implored God to reveal His loving intentions amidst this catastrophic event.

A few years have passed, and my dear friend glows with the knowledge of God's constancy, immediacy, and lovingkindness in her life. Yes, she is still pierced at the point from the great loss, but above, below, amidst, and at the bottom of that healing wound is her unshakable knowledge that God remains good. She has come a long way toward acceptance and knows that God, indeed, works all things out for best. She and her husband can give the deepest comfort and compassion now to others who suffer.

Doubting God's goodness is essentially what keeps most people from believing He exists and embracing Jesus as Savior and Lord. There are questions about personal suffering, war, or poverty. The list is long. I can't answer all the questions—or any of them for that matter—hurled heavenward about "Why didn't God stop this or that?"

When the kindness of God is at last glimpsed, life's questions and answers are trivial.

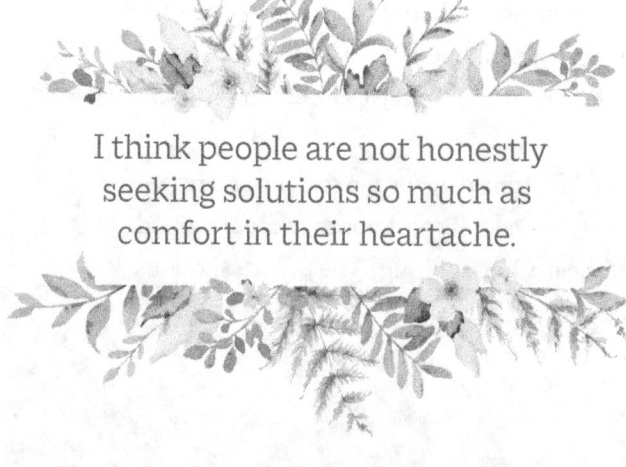

I think people are not honestly seeking solutions so much as comfort in their heartache.

What matters most is a foundation of belief in God's goodness and love amidst the most horrific events.

God's Word is replete with messages and examples of His loving character. Bottom line, I choose to believe them. I don't have answers for suffering, but amidst it, I seek and inquire about His goodness every day. The Good Shepherd reveals He cares in many tender, small, and large ways.

It is OK to struggle with knowing if God is good. He is not threatened by doubts. But God will allow a person to remain outside of the knowledge of His goodness if the doorway to His kindness is blocked by human doubt.

It takes a small step of faith—the kind you employ to drive over a bridge or use an elevator.

I love Corrie ten Boom's words from after she was forced to live in a concentration camp for hiding Jews in her home in Holland: "There is no pit so deep that Jesus' love is not deeper still."[14]

Now, that is a woman who found the goodness of God despite injustices and trials in her life. After World War II she spent the rest of her life declaring to the world that God is good!

ROAD MAP TO JOY

Scripture
"I remain confident of this: I will see the goodness of the Lord in the land of the living" (Ps. 27:13).

Prayer
Dear Lord, open Your living Word so I may know Your goodness in my suffering. Enable me to taste and see that You are good and working for my good all the time.

Activation
Create a list of your favorite scriptures displaying God's goodness. Read them daily so they become part of the fabric of your thinking. Express thanksgiving for His blessings. List them as well. You become what you meditate upon. God's generous goodness is as close as you will allow Him to come to you. Your life will overflow with joy when you begin to glimpse how He can be trusted amid life's heartaches.

Further Study
Exodus 34:6, Psalm 23:6, and Mark 10:18

> *For the Present is the point at which time touches eternity.*
>
> —C. S. LEWIS

29

First Rain

Sometimes the rain
carries me to the eternal
God Himself whose

shadow He deigned
to shimmer within a
fading fragment—

like a raindrop. When
heaven and earth blend,
the atmosphere grows

redolent with eternity.
One small picture of
that mix is rain and earth.

First rain mingled with
soil takes on irresistible
scent. Before the heavens

the aroma is heavy and
captivating: but there is a
compelling,

earthy yet ethereal quality
when water from
heaven *first* touches

the dirt of earth.
Those initial few drops of
downpour fusing with

common soil is bursting
with life, with potential.
That aromatic blend—earth and

first rain mingled—is one fraction
of forever: A symbol of eternity.
It is a withering moment that says,

"Heaven and earth are inextricably
bound, and God created us and
intends for us to live forever."

God uses withering moments
and events to point to things
that will last forever.

ROAD MAP TO JOY

I grew up in Colorado and visited the mountains often. A favorite memory was watching the clouds churn up a storm as the sky grew dark, waiting for the clouds to release. The first drops are sometimes large splashes against the window. I remember stepping outside and smelling first rain. It has an ethereal quality—the mixing of soil and water from heaven. It brought me joy as a child and still does!

Scripture
"Yet he has not left himself without testimony: He has shown kindness by giving you rain from heaven and crops in their seasons; he provides you with plenty of food and fills your hearts with joy" (Acts 14:17).

Prayer
I thank You, Lord, that the very rain falling from heaven is testimony of Your kindness and provision.

Activation
The rain points to God as the provider and shows His kindness. It should prove His existence and underscore it in your life. When it rains, pause to thank Him and wonder at the miracle of it. Rain has been given to bring you joy. Receive it as such.

Further Study
Joel 2:23, Job 5:10, and Deuteronomy 11:14

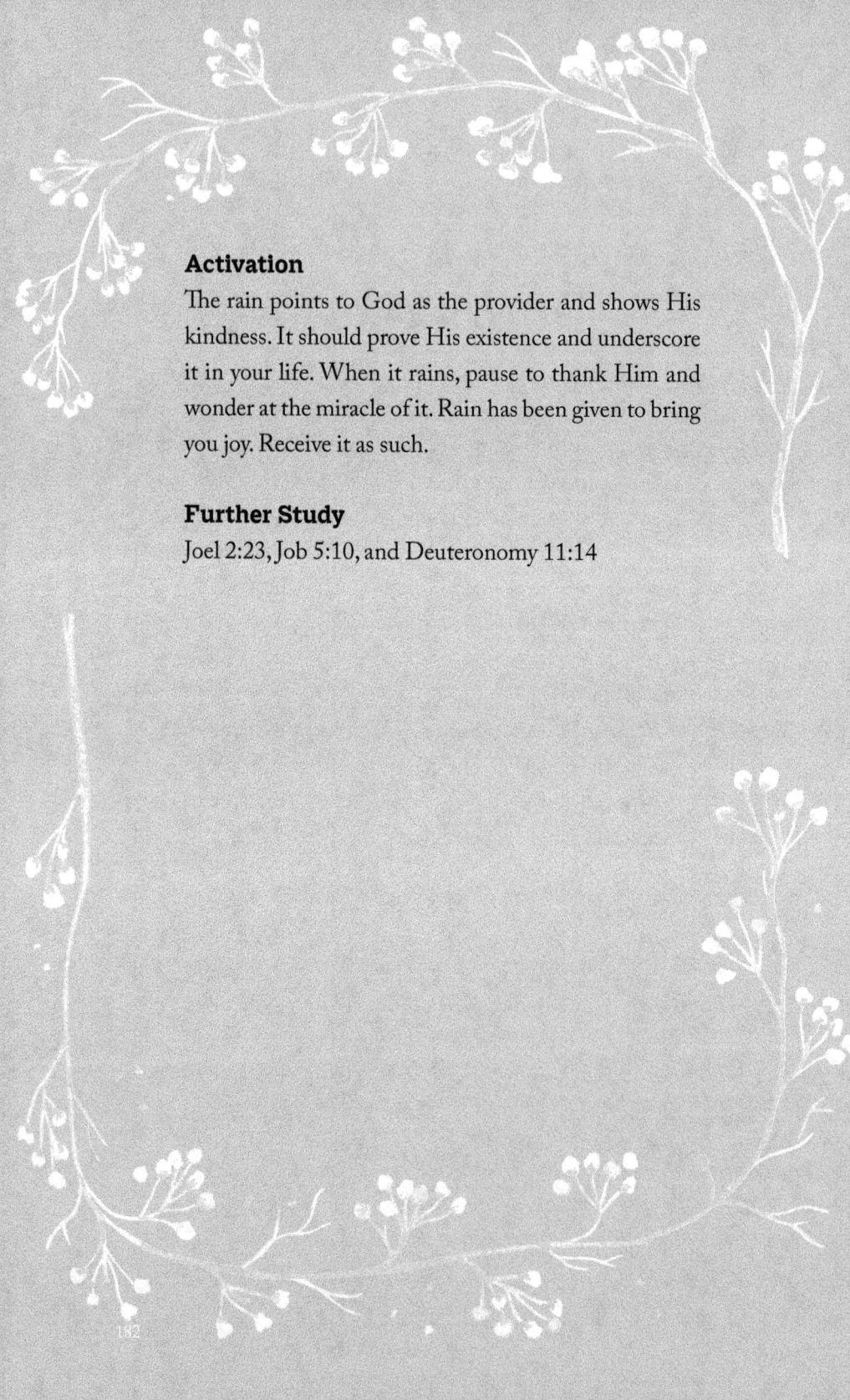

Hope is one of the Theological virtues. This means that a continual looking forward to the eternal world is not (as some modern people think) a form of escapism or wishful thinking, but one of the things a Christian is meant to do.

—C. S. LEWIS

30

She Hoped

In Hebrew, *she* is *he*, and *he* is *who*, and *who* is *he*, and *me* is *who*. Confusing? Maybe, and maybe not.

Now, with that said, I still believe Hebrew is one of the easiest languages in the world to learn. Here's why: Its grammar construction is simple and logical and has only three tenses. Maybe God made it straightforward because He knew immigrants from all over the world would return someday to their land and need to assimilate quickly by learning the language.

The big challenge in learning Hebrew is relearning the direction from left to right to right to left. Now begin on a clean slate with different symbols and do an about-face, moving your hand in the other direction. Once you get that—and it can be learned—then you are off to a great foundation of comprehension!

Rich, colorful, and filled with spiritual depth, Hebrew is a fascinating language.

I have spent many years of my adult life uncovering the treasured meanings buried within the root system. Like the Energizer batteries, Hebrew root definitions just keep giving and giving. They are so helpful in understanding the Bible.

Here is one example from my experience of living on a kibbutz in Israel in my early twenties.

I walked slowly to work that first morning. As I headed toward the general dining hall and kitchen on Kibbutz Einat, near Petah Tikva, Israel, I practiced these words over and over, "*Ani ovedet poe ha yom*," which means, "I work here today" in Hebrew.

My legs quivered with weakness, and huge butterflies flapped against the walls of my stomach as I approached my workspace for the day. I tried to analyze why I was hyperventilating as I walked. Oh yeah! I had never worked a job in another language or country. I had never had to understand and carry out instruction in a tongue other than English. Unlike many of my American comrades working as volunteers, I alone had been assigned to a job. Absolutely alone. I had no friends with whom to share the terror!

I saw the cook, Chaya, waiting for me just inside the large kitchen door. With all the courage I could muster, I stepped over the threshold and mumbled out my Hebrew words. Chaya grabbed my face with both hands, stroked my head and hair over and over (a very Eastern European and sweet Jewish gesture), and exclaimed in Hebrew, "I am so glad you speak Hebrew!" I gulped and faked it through my first day.

I knew just enough Hebrew to be dangerous. I had studied for two years formally before arriving in Israel. I had learned in the sterile environment of a classroom, which was entirely different from the situation in which I suddenly found myself.

Soon I enrolled in an ulpan—a Hebrew language school for new immigrants. The ulpan method of learning language is considered one of the best in the world. Since new immigrants in Israel come from many countries, the common language in an ulpan is strictly Hebrew, no lapsing into Russian, English, Romanian, Yiddish, or pig latin—nothing!

Ulpan is not for the faint of heart. To survive, you must jump into the rough, white-water rapids of guttural "chas" and rolled "rrrrrrs," knowing the waterfall of fluency is a few miles downriver. Once you get over the shocking cold water of embarrassment, you must paddle, paddle, paddle with strange syllables, diphthongs, and triphthongs. Then, when the waterfall finally comes, just let go and free fall, all in Hebrew!

It's super fun when you start laughing at your own mistakes. You might as well because everyone else is!

Although guttural, Hebrew is a beautiful language. When the adjectives, verbs, and nouns agree, the poetic sounds and rhythms abound. I love to hear a native speaker. It sounds like a blend of French and Portuguese with a hint of German. And oh, how I love the romantic sounds of French. I have always said that if I am going to be martyred, let it be by a Frenchman.

All words are based on a three-letter root system, although there are some irregularities. From these three letters, all words are formed. Unlocking the codes to these DNAs found in Hebrew roots is like finding a buried treasure chest. Since you cannot separate language from culture, it is advantageous to learn some Hebrew if you want to better understand the Bible or the life and times of Jesus.

Here are the roots of two words that I find interesting. *Zachar* is taken from the Hebrew root *remember*, from which the word *masculine* is derived. *Kava* is taken from the Hebrew root *hope*, from which the word *feminine* is derived. The very core of masculine in Hebrew literally means "to remember." The very depth of feminine in Hebrew is "to hope."

In Hebrew thought, the essence of being masculine means to remember God, to remember responsibility, to remember family. Scripture verifies this in Micah 6:8 (NKJV): "He has shown you, O man, what *is* good; And what does the LORD require of you but to do justly, to love mercy, and to walk humbly with your God?" Man must remember.

Conversely, the woman is created to hope in her God, to hope in her husband, and to hope for the lives of her children. Her hope is geared to the present and launches forward into the future, but is centered on God, her husband, and family. Proverbs 31:25 (ESV) says, "Strength and dignity are her clothing, and she laughs at the time to come." The woman who puts her hope in God first learns to have no fear for tomorrow.

These attributes create tension between the masculine and feminine: remembering versus hoping. It seems God set it up that way!

ROAD MAP TO JOY

There is so much gender confusion in our world. Modern men are emasculated, and women have become vile and dominate. This saddens me. The Holy Spirit seems to be whispering the foundation of masculine and feminine roles through the root meaning of their names, *zachar* and *kavah* —he remembered and she hoped. I long to be the woman of faith who hopes in her God and laughs at the future because she knows her faith is firm. I long to be married to a man who remembers his God and his duty to his wife and family. It is such a beautiful thought that God created man and woman as living examples of hope and remembrance of Him. When men and women find their rightful and ordained-by-God place, it allows rivers of peace, hope, and joy to flow through the heart and through the journey.

Scripture
"May the God of all hope fill you with all joy and peace in believing, so that by the power of the Holy Spirit you may abound in hope" (Rom. 15:13, ESV).

Prayer

Dear Lord, help me experience God's fullness of joy and peace, which leads to abundant hope.

Activation

God gives many gifts—joy and peace—which ultimately lead to hope. The Father's desire for you is to live with confidence in His love and plan for your life so you overflow with hope. If you have lost hope, begin to express your disappointments or sufferings to a trusted friend, pastor, or professional. You need not walk alone as you begin to rebuild and hope again.

Further Study

Jeremiah 29:11, Romans 8:24–25, and 1 Peter 1:3

Recommended Reading

The Tongue of the Prophets by Robert St. John, a history of the modern revival of the Hebrew language, and *Adventures in Prayer: A 40-Day Journey* by Mary Jo Pierce

In commanding us to glorify Him, God is inviting us to enjoy Him.

—C. S. LEWIS

31

Where Flowers Crack the Stone

Deep in the thick green
shimmering isle,
I'll plant with care
ancient seeds
carried in my womb.
I'll lavish them upon
the rich soil between
narrow, winding roads
and rolling, sheep-laden
pastures—upon the
moss-grown cliffs
where the flowers
crack the stone
to bloom for strength

of life and strength
of beauty—along the
shining coasts where
the fishermen lived
and died by the sea, where
the wild horse galloped
the shore. The seed-
dreams of my forefathers
have come full-circle—
beyond the door of green,
laden with
storytellers and poets,
lovers and fighters.
I'll pour water from
the ancient wells upon
seeds and weep for joy
as I walk the old
circular pathway,
carved in stone and
wrapping the cross of
eternal blood-soaked
triumph. "Church, teach
the cross" the Gaelic
imperative translates the
Celtic symbol. The lily
trumpeters across the
land declare, "Awake,
oh, Ireland, awake!" That
He who died, did not
in vain and the sleeping
seed arouses to reclaim

the dreams of the straight
Irish old, born anew of
water and of blood.

—*Dublin, Ireland*

ROAD MAP TO JOY

My husband, daughter, and I relished a seven-day road trip across the Emerald Isle, Ireland. It was too short but long enough to make us long to return and open our eyes to the spiritual wealth of the Irish—as beautiful as the glittering green land itself. As we drove along the coastland and upon the stony, majestic cliffs, we witnessed hundreds upon hundreds of lavish wildflowers breaking through the rocks to bloom "by strength of life and love." I wrote this poem as we drove, imagining God's love for this nation and its people—how our Redeemer has revealed Himself to the Irish throughout history and how, even now, Jesus, Savior, calls them to walk the circular pathway back to the cross.

Scripture
"Here I am! I stand at the door and knock. If anyone hears my voice and opens the door, I will come in and eat with that person and they with me" (Rev. 3:20).

Prayer
Dear Lord, give me a heart that is soft and yearns for the salvation of every person, every nation on earth. Please reveal yourself to those sitting in darkness. Please make me sensitive and bold enough to share my faith with others.

Activation
Remember the circumstances of your salvation. Did someone pray for you or with you? Be aware of opportunities to pray with family, friends, and neighbors, or share how God has been good to you.

Further Study
John 14:21–23, Mark 16:15, and Matthew 28:19

Recommended Reading
Is That Really You God?: Hearing the Voice of God by Loren Cunningham, and *Taking Our Cities for God* by John Dawson

In the moral sphere, every act of justice or charity involves putting ourselves in the other person's place and thus transcending our own competitive particularity.

—C. S. LEWIS

32

Want to Even the Score?

I blinked in disbelief and asked the woman to repeat. "Yes," her eyes twinkled as she spoke, "your tuition has been paid in full." "Paid in full?" I questioned—hardly able to take it in.

It was a random act of kindness, and the ripple effect of it shattered the core of disbelief that had been growing in my heart.

After licensed practical nurse training in Denver, I worked and saved money to attend Bible school. I knew Christian leadership training would complete the circle of preparation for the calling I sensed for the future. When it came time to depart, I left with enough money for one semester. And I thanked the Lord for it. The money was more than most students had upon entering the two-year ministry school located in Dallas, Texas.

I struggled financially during the first year and made ends meet by working part-time as a nurse. You can imagine my utter joy and surprise when I entered the administrative headquarters to discuss payment for the second year, and the registrar told me my bill had been paid in full by an anonymous donor.

I didn't walk home to my dorm room; I floated and walked on air for the next semester. Who could have done such a kind thing? And why me? That generous gift changed my life.

I learned something sweet about my heavenly Father. I felt His love in a tangible way. I *knew* He cared and was actively involved in my life. I also learned something about myself. Previously, I felt shortchanged. Various circumstances in the past had quietly robbed my hope and joy for the future. My thoughts were inaccurate and originated from the father of lies, though they seemed very real.

That great gift—a random act of kindness—somehow evened the score of the past. I know it is strange, but it brought clarity to some things for which I had questioned God. Even though I mistakenly blamed Him and my thinking was twisted, God used an anonymous donor to show His love. I felt like I had started life with a clean slate. As the Scripture says, "I forgot the things of the past and pressed on to that upward calling in Christ Jesus" (Phil. 3:14).

I have other examples in life as well that did the same thing. God's greatest gift to me is my husband. I am amazed that my heavenly Father would give me such a wonderful life partner. His leadership and love have constantly proven the promises of God are true and faithful, and the lies of the devil are full of hot air.

The adoption of my precious daughter from Guatemala and the joy of her life also proves to me every day that God is faithful and the Father of Lights continues to give treasures to His children.

On the other hand, giving random acts of kindness blesses my socks off. It truly exceeds receiving. Once, I paid the bill for a woman who stood in line behind me at the grocery store. She appeared to be struggling financially and had three crying children at her feet—her face clouded with hopelessness.

Quietly I gave the cashier enough cash to cover the woman's items. I didn't stay to see what happened, but I cried all the way home for the sheer joy of giving. A burst of purpose exploded in my heart. I found it contagious and yearned to do it again.

My pleasure most likely exceeded the woman's surprise of happiness. But I bet, that random act of kindness helped even the score in a small way for the injustices she had endured in life—or at least helped smooth down the roughness.

Injustice keeps us from God. Both believers and nonbelievers often ask the same questions about why God allows suffering or injustice. I have worked with Jewish Holocaust survivors around the world. The severity of their suffering and loss has caused some to stop believing in God's justice. If the Lord of heaven is not just, then He does not love either. I do not minimize their reactions to such heinous crimes perpetrated against the Jewish people during World War II.

One of the best books ever written about the injustices of the Holocaust is *Night* by Elie Wiesel. His recollections bound off the pages from his personal and historical documentation of that living hell—one whose screams shriek to this day from the scorched land and the scarred lives of survivors. The brutality of such inhumane acts and the loss of innocent life grieved my soul deeply. The horrors grew more ghastly, more demonic, and the story ended in unresolved hopelessness.

Brushing tears from my eyes, compassion rose in my heart as I closed the small book. My bones ached with the inability to change circumstances for the Wiesel family, for the whole Jewish nation. One statement from *Night* pierced my heart above the others:

> Never shall I forget that night, the first night in camp, which has turned my life into one long night, seven times cursed and seven times sealed.[15]

It is hard to wrap my mind around the anguish and despair that drove a man to write such words. As I read, my heart longed for justice, which would cancel the darkness and the curse.

Later, I saw a journalist interview Wiesel. She asked him, "Can you draw some good from this experience?" He shook his head no. Wiesel had lost his faith.

Faith and justice must exist side by side. There will not be justice if faith dies. Conversely, there will not be faith if injustice goes unpunished. It is so intertwined that Jesus used it in a parable in Luke 18 about the woman who persuades the judge by pleading for justice. Because she does not let up, he grants her request.

> Two things stand out from this strong illustration about faith and justice:
>
> 1. We are not to avenge ourselves. God is the righteous judge, and His very name is Justice. He will right the injustices on the earth, but we must plead for it relentlessly as the widow did.
>
> 2. We must not lose our faith as we wait for His justice. Thus, the question at the end of the parable, "Will the Son of Man find faith on the earth when He returns?" He *will* find justice, but will He find faith?

Bringing justice in life is not the problem, because God's very nature is just. Keeping faith while we wait on God's timing is.

The ministry that my husband and I served reached out to Jewish Holocaust survivors regularly. In Ukraine, we have provided feeding programs and aid. Students of the Messianic Jewish Bible Institute brought food and medicines into the homes of survivors. They sat and talked with the recipients and eventually found open doors to discuss Jesus as the Jewish Messiah. They explained the good news in Jewish context, and many embraced redemption.

It brings us joy to make an eternal difference in Jewish people's lives because they have suffered through the Holocaust so unjustly. These changed lives started with the small act of kindness of bringing a meal to the home of a poor Holocaust survivor.

Random or planned acts of kindness can help even the score in the lives of others. They open their heart to hear and receive salvation. They heal scars and restore people's faith in the goodness of God.

> Extended kindness through acts of love becomes a significant signpost on life's rough road that points to heaven instead of eternal destruction.

I don't want to minimize the need for rightful justice. That is why the world brought Nazi leaders to trial and punished them. The need to even the score will never end in this life. God cares about justice more than we do. He also cares that faith remains strong. I prayed for Elie Wiesel—for justice and his faith to be restored, for God's people to show him kindness so he may believe.

ROAD MAP TO JOY

While writing this, I am inspired to reexamine how kindness around me helps alleviate the pain of injustice. I believe God is showing me His love over and over. I also know I have the power to help someone else see that God is reaching out to them through small yet significant kindnesses. As a person who loves justice and wants to see the wrongs of life righted, I am really jazzed that God has given me the power to help even the score through a simple act of kindness.

Scripture
"This is what the Lord Almighty said: 'Administer true justice; show mercy and compassion to one another. Do not oppress the widow or the fatherless, the foreigner or the poor. Do not plot evil against each other'" (Zech. 7:9–10).

Prayer
Dear Lord, thank You for your kindness to me. Help me recognize it in the daily flow of my life, and allow those actions to soften my heart toward You.

Activation

In the darkest pages of history, God is revealing His light through the kindness of others. Sometimes it is easy to miss these gifts from a loving Father because we are awaiting grand deliverance from our trials and suffering. In the painful season of blind faith, a good God is at work, sending bursts of kindness through people and circumstances around us. He is softening our hearts to draw us away from His judgment and into His mercy. Reflect on the tiny kindnesses that have influenced your life and journal about them. Determine to pay kindness forward.

Further Study
Romans 2:4, Luke 6:35, and 1 Peter 4:8

Mercy, detached from Justice, grows unmerciful.

—C. S. LEWIS

33

Justice

S ociety demands vengeance but cannot bear justice, requires morality but cannot stand faultless under a searchlight, expects order but despises authority, screams for open borders and the acceptance of the tired, poor huddled masses yearning to be free but won't share a meal and offer a bed to a stranger in need.

We are not a collection
of savage tribesmen
surviving on the street
but a nation of divine
destiny. Rise by recognizing
the Creator, who is evident
in the universe, as God.
Rise by lifting others,
rise by relinquishing
rights. Rise to glorious
realms beyond this
earth to take your
place in His diadem.
King Jesus.
Only the righteous
understand justice, which
brings us to the subject
of blood.

ROAD MAP TO JOY

The pursuit of justice is serious and God inspired. It is important that humankind is afforded due process when they have been treated unjustly. Faith dies when justice is ignored or unnecessarily delayed. Nothing steals my joy more than witnessing or experiencing wrong treatment without retribution. It helps to remember that Jesus shed His blood unjustly so there can be justice in the earth and heaven. The acts of injustice must answer to higher authority, and often we must wait for the wheels of local law, which sometimes move slowly. There are things we can do to help bring justice on the earth. I wrote this poem with that thought in mind.

Scripture
"Justice never makes sense to men devoted to darkness, but those tenderly devoted to the Lord can understand justice perfectly" (Prov. 28:5–6, TPT).

Prayer

I thank You, Lord, that You love justice, so much that Your courts in heaven are named "Justice" (Ps. 89:14). Give me Your perspective of godly justice. Help me understand and embrace it. Show me how I can live justly and love justice in an unjust world.

Activation

Is there something unjust that has happened to you that caused you to lose faith in God or people? If so, begin to cry out to God for justice and pray about this earnestly. God wants you to seek Him first and wait patiently for His retribution. Waiting for God's justice brings joy.

Further Study

Jeremiah 4:22, Psalm 25:14, and Proverbs 15:24

We might think that God wanted simply obedience to a set of rules: whereas He really wants people of a particular sort.

—C. S. LEWIS

34

The What, When, and How of Obedience

Tears streamed down my face, and my legs shook as I listened to her story, describing the death and martyrdom of her beloved husband. At age fourteen I heard the account of Jim Elliot and the four missionaries who were savagely killed in South America by a tribe called the Auca Indians.

Elisabeth Elliot, his widow, came to my home church, Calvary Temple, in Denver, Colorado, to give her testimony. Her message of love, forgiveness, and sacrifice impacted my life. As Elliot traveled across states, hundreds, maybe thousands, dedicated their lives, to serving God more fully at home and abroad.

Even as a teenager I recognized the power and calling of God to surrender my life to His will.

My immediate response to the Holy Spirit's beckoning was emotional, but my resolve was body, soul, and spirit—and I remained firm. As I prepared for ministry through nurse's training and Bible school, I never forgot this experience. Elisabeth Elliot's story and the glimpse of God's glory and love for mankind bloomed in my heart the day she spoke.

After Bible school I went to Israel to live on a kibbutz. I stayed two and a half years, attended language school, developed significant friendships, and learned to love the people of the Middle East—both Arabs and Jews. After returning to the United States, I married and adopted a baby girl. My husband and I longed to be used abroad to help reveal the Messiah to Jewish people.

During those years of equipping and waiting, we constantly asked the Lord, "What do you have for us beyond the local church?" and "When will we be released?" We desperately loved our congregation and community, yet we knew we had to be released one day. In 1996, our pastor and leadership team sent us out with blessings to begin the first Messianic Jewish Bible Institute, a Bible school for Messianic believers in Jesus in Odesa, Ukraine.

The flames of Communism had gone underground, and teams carrying the good news of salvation streamed into the country. Thousands began to turn their lives toward Him. It was harvesting time! We finally realized the *what* and *when* of our calling.

What we did not prepare for was waiting upon the *how*. As we started the school, adding students and settling into the city, we hit wall after wall. The journey seemed like we were taking half a step forward and then five steps backward. The spiritual warfare hit us like a tidal wave, and suddenly, we were surrounded by many critics, naysayers, and a few sheep in wolves' clothing—sometimes our own brethren.

We felt betrayed and bewildered by the barrage of constant opposition. Still, we pressed on, even maybe when we should have waited and asked God, "How should we proceed?" I think our zeal to enjoy the *what* and *when* overtook the importance of *how*.

As I remember this journey today, I am reminded of David bringing the Ark of the Covenant to Jerusalem in 2 Samuel 6. His intentions were pure and righteous, and his timing was in tune with the movement of the Holy Spirit. David heard God, but he did not wait to hear the how. That mistake cost time and human life.

Uzzah died as the Ark began to be moved. It slipped—Uzzah grabbed the sacred object that belonged in the Holy of Holies as it teetered, and he fell to his death (2 Sam. 6:6–7).

After this shocking event, David rested the Ark at Obed-Edom's home for three months before finally proceeded finally to Jerusalem. Only this time the Levites carried the Ark and moved only six steps at a time before making sacrifices to the Lord. What an intensely and agonizingly slow journey. But as they obeyed God's *how*, David danced, and the people praised and shouted. The Ark finally arrived at its resting place with great victory and the sounds of horns blasting. The *how* became as significant as the *what* and *when*.

ROAD MAP TO JOY

Sometimes following God's way or timing causes us to move painfully slow or stops us mid-project. But the purpose is to instill within us a healthy dose of God's fear, which is the foundation of all wisdom, as we begin to fulfill our destinies in the Lord's will.

Scriptures
"When those who were carrying the ark of the Lord had taken six steps, he sacrificed a bull and a fattened calf" (2 Sam. 6:13).

"The fear of the Lord leads to life; then one rests content, untouched by trouble" (Prov. 19:23).

Prayer
Dear Lord, help me see You as the Bible describes, full of power, dominion, majesty, and might. Help me fear You in a healthy way. I know this fear will bring wisdom into my life as I seek to please and live for You.

Activation
Seeking God's perfect will for your life takes patient endurance. Sometimes the greatest test comes when we discover those things but don't wait to discover the *how* of our callings. God is always good and desires for us to prosper in His will, but as He works with us, we must fear His ways. Take time to wait on God for the *hows* of accomplishing His will, even if it seems you are taking only six steps forward. Praise Him as David did with all his might for six steps; then make a sacrifice before you continue. This patient fear of God will save you from heartache in the long run.

Further Study
Exodus 25:10–16, Exodus 26:34, and Proverbs 10:27

35

The Frayed Hem

Earth's latitude and longitude run as high as humankind's intelligence
and as long and wide as our strength and life span.
Here we live caged.

We run the circled courses of these by the second—
up and down and
around—our machinations are profound. We are curing cancer and
changing sexes, flying beyond the moon and putting steak sauce on

grasshoppers. Everything is possible but the hemorrhaging rages on.

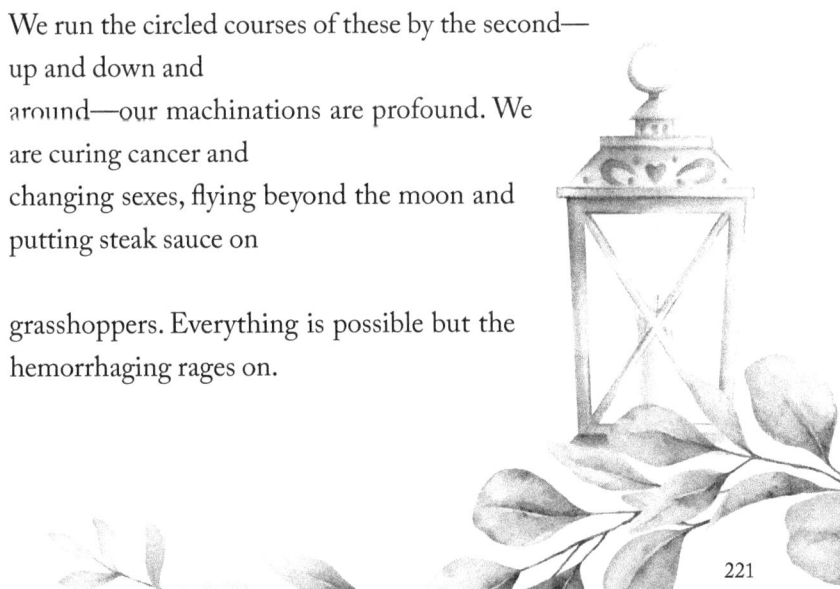

How smart we are! How cleverly calculated, until we blindly stumble
upon—to slip between—the thin edges of the circumference where

darkness is dispelled, and intimacy is sunny, warm, and understood.
Where all the whys free-fall between the graph lines.
Here, soaring to the stars and tuning our hearts to their songs is

possible. Here eternity is tangible and normal. Mystery is as unspeakable as joy. It's where we know that He exists and has always
existed and has placed the infinite in each heart. Here He has

hemmed me in—front and back,

side by side. Here I reach for the scarlet cord of life eternal and stretch
faith for the frayed hem that will stop my bleeding. Here I am broken and cloistered in the thin place. Here I am undone, falling upward.

ROAD MAP TO JOY

I can't tell you the number of times I have returned to Psalm 139 for comfort. Often the world is strange, and I feel out of place in it. The psalm, however, is grounding and life-giving, inspiring me to write poems such as the one above. It brings me great joy to know that my Creator God is intimately aware of the depths of my heart, longings, failings, fears, hopes, and dreams.

Scripture
"You have searched me, Lord, and you know me. You know when I sit and when I rise; you perceive my thoughts from afar. You discern my going out and my lying down; you are familiar with all my ways. Before a word is on my tongue you, Lord, know it completely. You hem me in behind and before, and you lay your hand upon me. Such knowledge is too wonderful for me, too lofty for me to attain" (Ps. 139:1–6).

Prayer
I am thankful that You know me, Lord. You are familiar with my thoughts, fears, and frustrations. You do not condemn but long to offer me pathways of joy no matter my circumstances. I reach out for Your deliverance and plan. I ask for help and direction, knowing You love me and have my best in mind always.

Activation
Describe a place where you feel safe, seen, and understood. Why do you feel safe? If that place is not grounded in an intimate relationship with Jesus, how can you change it?

Further Study
Hebrews 4:13, Jeremiah 12:3, and Psalm 17:3

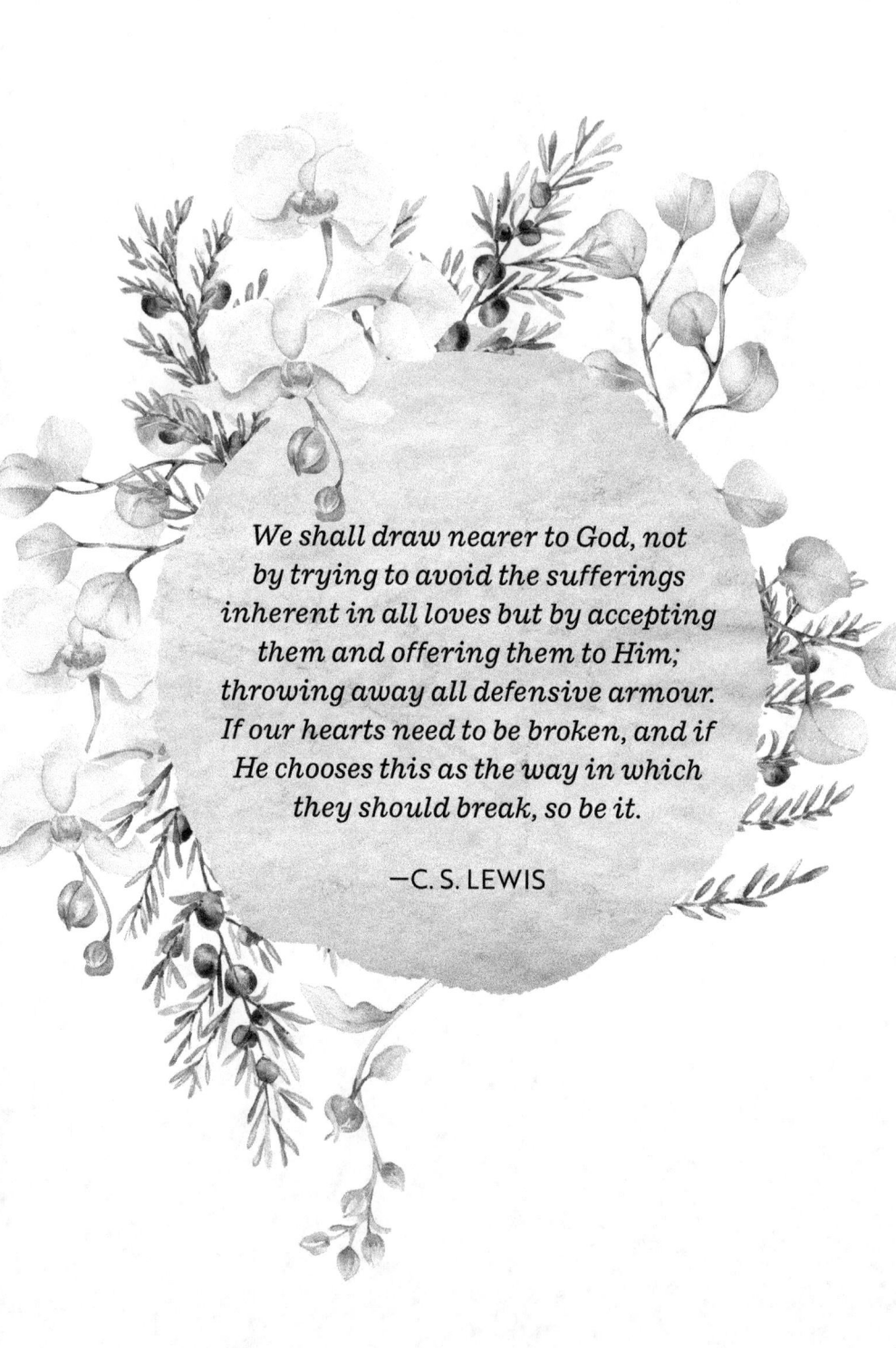

> We shall draw nearer to God, not by trying to avoid the sufferings inherent in all loves but by accepting them and offering them to Him; throwing away all defensive armour. If our hearts need to be broken, and if He chooses this as the way in which they should break, so be it.
>
> —C. S. LEWIS

36

You Intended to Harm Me

Impatience is to resist—mentally, emotionally, or even physically—a person or life event that we cannot control.

The Hebrew word for *patience* is *savlanut* (סַבְלָנוּת), coming from the simple root *samech-lamed-nun* (s-l-n). This root is connected by other words like *sevel* (סבל), meaning suffering; *lisbol* (לִסְבֹּל), meaning to suffer; *sivolet* (סִבֹּלֶת), meaning tolerance; and *sovel* (סובל), meaning burden, highlighting the complex relationship between patience and endurance in the Hebrew language.

There is a unifying thread weaving through these Hebraic words, which helps us understand patience. As we see in the life of Joseph, he developed into a man of great patience through a myriad of life-changing evil schemes, deceptions, years of suffering, and agonizing delays (Gen. 40–41).

He suffered hardships and became tolerant as he bore unjust burdens. I imagine his reaction amid these events was not perfectly ideal, rather normal, like you or me.

I admire Joseph so much—through family betrayal, setbacks, and deception, he kept his eyes fixed on God the Deliverer. He experienced divine favor and grace as he allowed patience to transform arduous periods of waiting into times of unique fruitfulness. Even in prison, Joseph interpreted dreams, demonstrating that faithfully waiting can lead to unexpected and glorious opportunities. I believe he was an exemplary prisoner. He didn't have a rotten attitude while he waited for justice. He made his life good by reaching out to others, working hard, and maintaining compliance rather than resistance.

In time God rescued Joseph and gave him a position of favor, influence, and great wealth. Despite being a captive in a foreign land, he thrived and became a blessing to both the Egyptian and Hebrew people.

ROAD MAP TO JOY

Joseph said, "You meant evil against me; but God meant it for good…to save many people alive" (Gen. 50:20, NKJV). Joseph's life showcased how God transformed adversity into justice and redemption for his family and an entire nation. I have often imagined the rejection that a young Jewish boy felt when betrayed by his brothers—he must have felt abandoned by God as well. Always inspired by his story of faith and fortitude, I take great pleasure in reading over and over his account of the God who always sees, is working to intervene, and makes a way of escape in the midst of great darkness and disappointment.

Scripture
"You intended to harm me, but God intended it all for good. He brought me to this position so I could save the lives of many people" (Gen. 50:20, NLT).

Prayer
Dear Lord, give me patience. Help me not to be overcome with the burdens of today or uncertainties of tomorrow. Shower me with grace and acceptance as I surrender my will and life to You.

Activation
If you find yourself impatient during events out of your control, meditate on Joseph's life. Ask God to show you how, while waiting, you can become as viable and fruitful as Joseph. Don't internalize your frustrations; express them to God in prayer and with a confidant. Often a friend's counsel can be a sweet encouragement as you develop tolerance and patience. Adopt this key verse as a life verse. Memorize and meditate on it daily as you walk through trying situations. Faith and joy will rise in your heart that God is still writing your story.

Further Study
1 Corinthians 13:4–5, Romans 8:25, and Psalm 37:7

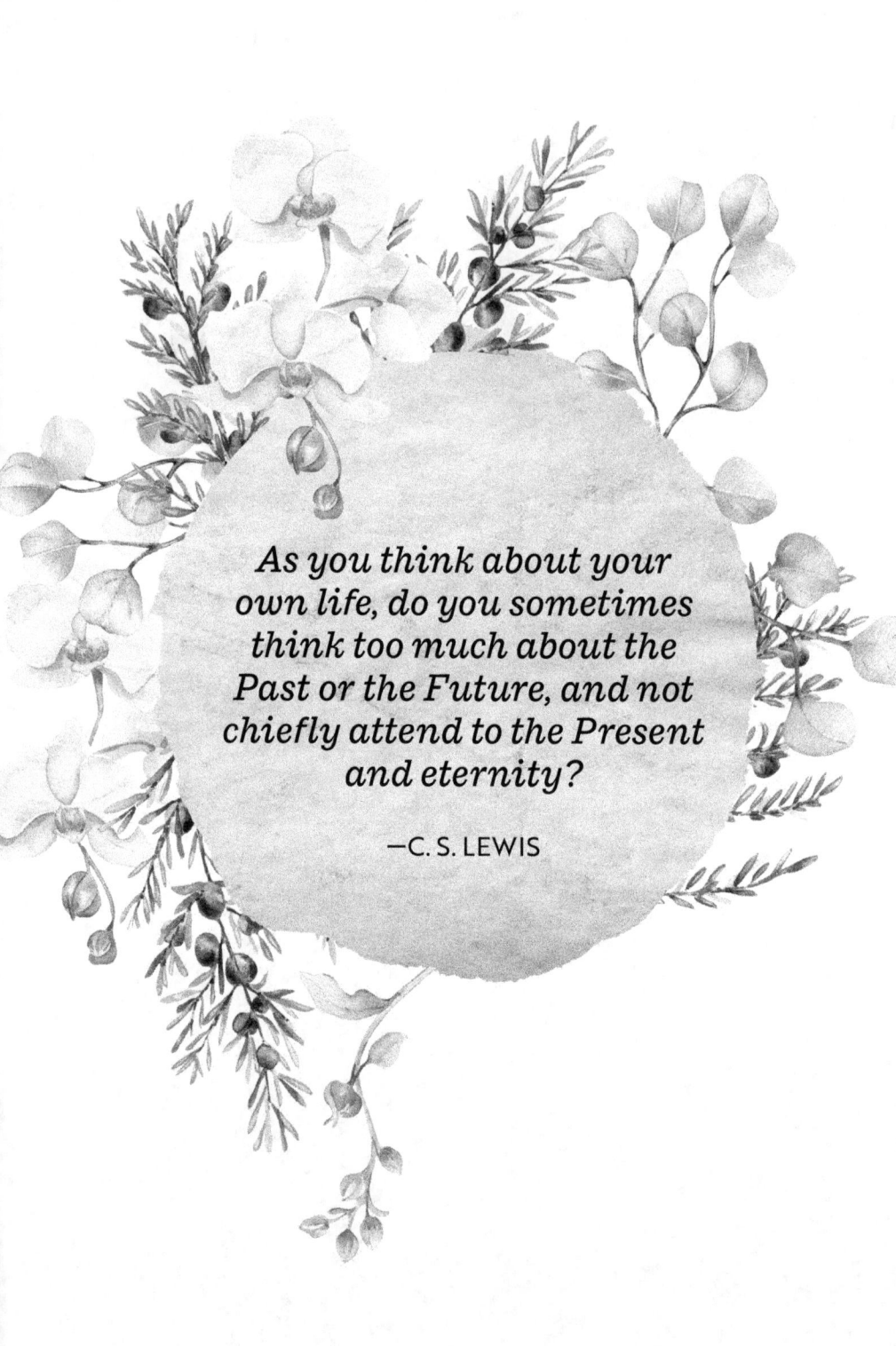

As you think about your own life, do you sometimes think too much about the Past or the Future, and not chiefly attend to the Present and eternity?

—C. S. LEWIS

37

Clocks in Argentina

In Buenos Aires, I am perched high
on the veranda of a small coffee bar.
A majestic cathedral
towers above me still, and I crane
my neck to survey its magnificent
spires. At the top, an alcove cradles
the sculpted body of a dead Jewish king.
His head, with a jeweled crown,
hangs in surrender,
while blood pours from His wounds.
Pigeons fly to and from the scarred image.

Huge clocks
surround the alcove crucifixion.
Three are visible from my vantage
point alone. Below me, madhouse

traffic rages like the insane, final
moments of a soccer game. This city
sanctuary offers a cup of tranquility for
five minutes of my time.

I accept the invitation of respite, from
the shadowed niche.

I close my eyes to imagine
the basilica—the stone, cold floor, and the
glowing warmth of candles, dozens
of them. Sanctuary gold and jewels
sparkle there. A priest's robe sways
across the room, incense fills the air, but the
candles command my attention.
They can be extinguished by a gust of
city wind, like my life's burden in an
amnesiac drop of Lamb's blood.

I wonder in awe
that I am sprung from those sculpted bloody
wounds in the darkened cubicle, and I
wonder what time it is.

ROAD MAP TO JOY

I loved it as a child and treasure it now even more as an adult—Robert Frost's famous poem "Stopping by Woods on a Snowy Evening." Every responsible adult can relate to Frost's verses, stopping to breathe and admire silent beauty after a long, hard day with miles to go.

That is exactly how I felt in Buenos Aires, Argentina, when I wrote this poem. Wayne and I were there teaching in a Bible school and had a very busy schedule. During a free hour, I sat in a coffee shop to rest my feet, but it was my spirit that gleaned the most from those few holy moments of contemplation. The crazy and noisy traffic raged outside, yet the church in the middle of the city had open doors where invitation beckoned. I didn't need to go in to experience its momentary respite; I imagined it and had to shake myself back to reality because a tremendous peace fell upon my heart.

I loved the juxtaposition of the crucifix, with its eternal message, next to the huge clock—the swift passing of time and the idea of eternity through salvation, where there is no time. I found my cup of peace had morphed into joy during those fleeting moments while taking time to reflect on the scene before me.

Scripture
"So teach us to number our days, that we may present to You a heart of wisdom" (Ps. 90:12, NASB).

Prayer
Dear Lord, open my eyes to see and embrace the brevity of life on earth. I ask for Your wisdom to live my days with prudence and sobriety so that they may count in heaven.

Activation
Too much focus on current disappointments and hardships in life—past, present, or future—leads to worry and fear, robbing one of peace and joy. It is lifesaving to comprehend that God's focus is entirely different. He is not restricted by resources, time, or our hardships. Seek a godly perspective of your circumstances and what eternal value they may have. God's purposes are truly everlasting. He gives wisdom liberally to those who ask. His all-knowing and merciful perspective makes us sober and joyful about each day as it comes.

Further Study
Psalm 39:4, Deuteronomy 30:9, and Ecclesiastes 7:2

Relying on God has to begin all over again every day as if nothing had yet been done.

—C. S. LEWIS

38

Sabbath as a Bride

The Sabbath is compared with a bride, coming to the people of God in purity and sanctity. Many *Shabbat* rituals surround this thought. Sixteenth-century mystics created the Friday evening service, known in Hebrew as *Kabbalat Shabbat*, which means "welcoming the Sabbath." During service the song *L'kah Dodi* is often sung:

> Come, my beloved, to meet the bride.
> Let us welcome the presence of the Sabbath
> Come in peace…and come in joy…
> Come, O Bride! Come, O Bride![16]

Today in Jewish Orthodox settings, as the last verse of the song is sung, the congregation will turn away from the ark housing the Torah and bow before the synagogue entrance as if the bride of Shabbat were about to enter.

As believers, the idea of Sabbath as a pure bride finds a home in our hearts at the end of the verse in Leviticus 23:3: "It is a Sabbath to the Lord." We hold close and yet see beyond the Orthodox view of Sabbath being the bride as we embrace the new covenant idea that we have become the pure bride by Yeshua's blood. Therefore, we greet the Sabbath prepared to steal away with our beloved Bridegroom for the space of twenty-four hours.

The powerful draw of the prosaic and temporal is set aside, enabling us to peer into the eternal portals of heaven by honoring this commandment. Shabbat is a weekly honeymoon with the Bridegroom, who is our Creator and Maker, and it is a glimpse of our future with the Lord.

Rather than becoming paralyzed by rules, the Sabbath should evoke great joy and expectation, as a bride has on her wedding day. As Messiah's bride, we will be presented to God in righteousness without spot or blemish (Eph. 5:27). We separate the time of Shabbat to be alone with our Bridegroom in delightful exclusivity.

Scripture is replete with many beautiful pictures of the bride and Bridegroom captivated by each other in romance. Song of Songs, beginning to end, describes in detail the intimate relationship between the bride and Bridegroom.

Judaism, rich with history, tradition, and culture, fullheartedly embraces the idea of Israel as the bride prepared for the one and only true God. Hosea describes the depth of love God has and suffering He endures for His unfaithful bride. The same message of boundless love resounds throughout Scripture. It is clearly seen in the new covenant as we visualize and ponder the way Jesus reached out to the woman caught in adultery. This woman, who deserved to die according to the Law, is the most definitive and colorful example of the rebellious and undeserving bride, who is captivated and eventually changed by a loving and selfless Bridegroom.

Gary Wiens writes in his book titled *Bridal Intercession: Authority in Prayer Through Intimacy With Jesus*:

> You see, the so-called fairy tales of history really are true. The Prince really has kissed the girl, the humble handmaid really is the Princess, and the Beauty who has been under the spell of the poison apple really will be brought to life. The King will have His glorious bride, and the desires of His heart will be satisfied. The stories are clear and you'll find them throughout Scripture. Our God is a God in love, and His burning heart is the heart of a Bridegroom Who will not be dissuaded from His task. His zeal burns for the restoration of His people, and He will not relent until the broken woman, whose name is Jerusalem, shines forth in the way He intended, as a praise in all the earth [Isa. 62:7].[17]

INTERCESSORY PURPOSES

The strength and importance of prayer and intercession can never be overemphasized. Through the centuries God has used prayer warriors to battle for His purposes on earth. Abraham cried out to God on behalf of Sodom, even when he knew the city was thoroughly evil. God answered his prayer. Moses pleaded for Israel again and again, even offering his own life in return, and God responded with mercy. Habakkuk asked for God to fight against injustice, and Nehemiah dreamed about and interceded for the rebuilding of the temple.

Jesus is the supreme example of intercession, earnestly praying for His people, even those who ridiculed and betrayed Him. The life of Jesus is a living representation of intercession because He was perfect, pure, and sinless. He always obeyed and took time to be alone with the Father. That is where He rested and was rejuvenated. That is where He pleaded in intercession for the lost sheep of the house of Israel.

Today, God calls His bride to do the same and become an example of living intercession for a lost and hurting on earth.

Again, Gary Wiens speaks of the place of the bride in intercession:

> In the prophetic portrait called the book of Esther, He is inviting us to approach intercession through the doorway of romance, to dial up all His daring and passionate emotions, to tell Him all over again that we say "yes" to His proposals, that we choose Him again even as at the first. He wants us to presume upon His grace and mercy, to enter the Holy of Holies with confident boldness, knowing that His scepter of righteousness is always extended toward us, because He is a King in love and we are His bride![18]

As the bride of Messiah, when we engage in Sabbath-keeping practices, we find ourselves fulfilling God's intercessory purposes on earth. The act of keeping the Sabbath is a prophetic command to Israel, repeated throughout the ages, demonstrating that God has made a covenant with His people and will keep it.

Keeping the Sabbath becomes an intercessory prayer that resounds into eternity. Its language is heard without words, yet is voiced through our actions, showing that the Sabbath stands forever as a sign between God and man. Through both word and deed

God shows that He is our provider. There is a physical and spiritual Sabbath rest for those who will seek it. The observance and remembrance of the Sabbath reinforces these truths in a literal and weekly manifestation.

For Israel the Sabbath stands as a highway marker that God has kept His promises and will continue if the foundations of the earth remain and there are stars in the sky. As Messianic believers enter Sabbath rest, the act becomes an intercessory cry for the light of Yeshua to shine into darkness, illuminating the hearts of Jews around the world, revealing the truth of salvation through Christ.

An invitation to Sabbath rest rings throughout the universe as His people strike the first match, lighting the Sabbath candles, lifting the brimming cup of wine, and blessing the God of Israel on the evening separated unto the Bridegroom and bride alone.

RITUALLY SET APART

To underscore the Sabbath's spiritual significance, it is ritually set apart and begins with a festive Friday evening meal—a special event that reminds us that we are keeping covenant with God and entering a holy time. To believers in Messiah, Shabbat is a picture of the marriage supper of the Lamb, when Messiah's bride is united with her Beloved in heaven because of the blood sacrifice of Yeshua (Rev. 19:7).[19]

ROAD MAP TO JOY

Could it be that in the days of preparation—as the church comes together as one new man, Jew and gentile united from every nation, tribe, and tongue in anticipation of the Lord's return—keeping Shabbat will be restored to the whole church as a foretaste of the bride's glorious reunion with the Bridegroom?

As gentile believers who love Israel, we invite Jews we meet in our everyday lives to our Shabbat table. They accept our invitation and become renewed in their love for their Jewish roots, open to the message of Messiah, and even jealous that we celebrate the Sabbath. Could these evening meals together, Jew and gentile at the table lit with Sabbath lights and filled with Yeshua's love extended, be a foretaste of something in eternity when we celebrate as one new man?

Scripture
"Thus the heavens and the earth were completed in all their vast array. By the seventh day God had finished the work he had been doing; so, on the seventh day he rested from all his work. Then God blessed the seventh day and made it holy, because on it he rested from all the work of creating that he had done"(Gen. 2:1–3).

Prayer
Dear Lord, I receive the treasure of the Sabbath as a gift of rest. Help me learn to honor it and find true joy and refreshment in learning to stop routinely.

Activation
Learning to rest on the Sabbath begins at the beginning of the week. Look ahead and schedule your day off as you would an appointment. This may taste like bitter medicine at first, but with discipline you will see and feel the benefits for you and your family. Experience will teach you that this is the most joyful day of each week.

Further Study
Ezekiel 20:19–20, Isaiah 58:13–14, and Mark 2:23–28

Recommended Reading
Sabbath: A Gift of Time by Bonnie Saul Wilks, and *Breathe: Making Room for Sabbath* by Priscilla Shirer

You can't know. You can only believe—or not.

—C. S. LEWIS

To Hope

Such sweet suffering it is
to hope—as
close as a kiss,
as far as the stars,
hope shimmers on thin air.
Blown upon winter winds,
hope hangs immobile, suspended
between heaven and earth,
just above the sea.
Driven by the will
of ocean breezes,
hope swirls upon
churning waters.
It swoops and sails,
carried in the arms of
relentless crosswinds—

that batter, that beat—
until at last,
hope is
plunged into the
deep, swallowed
by ancient, angry sea depths,
where faith is at last born.

ROAD MAP TO JOY

After nearly five hundred days in captivity, the hostages of the heinous October 7 attack on Israel by Hamas shared some of their stories. The world tuned in, blinking in shock as they told of the horrors that unfolded day after day. My husband and I sat stuck to the computer, listening to the gruesome details of evil and inhumane cruelty. We couldn't imagine living through such revulsion. One young, single Israeli female captured our attention as she related her story. Woven within was prayer and hope, in turn, not giving up on God or the faith of her forefathers. She used the Hebrew word over and over, *kiviti, kiviti, kiviti* (קיוויתי), "I hoped, I hoped, I hoped."

When I heard her testimony, I suddenly remembered a poem I had written several years ago, and more than that, why I had written it—for something or someone in the future. Sometimes a poet may write something and not know the meaning completely as the words come together to form a thought. This young lady's captors treated her abominably without conscience or care, yet she continued to pray. Daily she dug hope up from the depths of the ocean bottom and commenced the nearly impossible task of allowing it to arise anew in her heart. Hope became faith in the darkness of the situation. Joy is found in the work of hoping against hope, when God meets us in the blackest and most painful moments. It is profound knowing this courageous heroine continued to pray until her release.

Scripture
"Hope deferred makes the heart sick, but a longing fulfilled is a tree of life" (Prov. 13:12).

Prayer
Dear Lord, give me the strength to continue praying and hoping when all is lost. Encourage me with Your presence and Your Word when I feel alone and forgotten—when it looks as if the unjust are winning life's battles.

Activation
When you feel hopeless about life or a situation, picture yourself digging up new hope from the depths of the ocean. Fix your eyes on Jesus, keep praying, and

remember God's good and faithful promises to you. Encourage yourself with the stories of others who have overcome hopeless circumstances.

Further Study
John 16:22, Proverbs 13:19, and Psalm 17:15

He died not for men, but for each man. If each man had been the only man made, He would have done no less.

—C. S. LEWIS

40

Death by Low Salt

My hand shook as I picked up the fork from the drawer. What? I can't lift a fork? It felt as if I were raising a steel skillet instead of a utensil. I had been weak and dizzy for several days. The symptoms started with the worst headache of my life. No pain medicine touched it. Miserable with throbbing, I remained in bed for four days. Nine days previously, I had started a juice fast, so I figured the headache and faintness came from releasing toxins through fasting.

I waited and prayed, with no relief, so I knew I needed to call the doctor. He immediately sent me to the emergency room, where a blood test revealed I had low sodium. All the juicing and fasting had washed away a significant amount of salt from my body. The doctor explained the seriousness of my condition, which could lead to convulsions, hallucinations, and even death.

In the ER I received saline water intravenously, and the doctor's parting words were, "You will feel weak and crummy for a few weeks, but go home and enjoy a bag of chips."

A slight smile crossed my face. How ironic, I thought—a doctor prescribing a bag of chips!

Health returned slowly, but recuperating gave me time to ask the Lord why this happened. His reply was sweet yet direct. "I didn't cause this, but I'm using it for your good." My interest was piqued; I looked up all verses on becoming salt and light to the world.

> You are the salt of the earth. But what good is salt if it has lost its flavor? Can you make it salty again? It will be thrown out and trampled underfoot as worthless.
> —Matthew 5:13, NLT

Then the Lord said, "You have lost your saltiness."

I knew it was true. It had been a long time since I witnessed to anyone about the life-transforming power of Jesus' blood. I just got busy and felt that because I had served as a missionary and church leader, I was doing my part interceding, traveling, writing, counseling, and teaching.

I repented of my lack of saltiness, and this life lesson showed me that it is possible to die, both physically and spiritually, if I don't actively maintain my sodium levels. Scripture declares, "Taste and see that the LORD is good!" (Ps. 34:8, ESV).

Sprinkling of the salt of the gospel is what makes people hungry and thirsty to know His love and goodness.

As I grew stronger physically, I grew bolder. I talked to everyone, just as I did when I first encountered Jesus' love and saving power. Sometimes I kept people waiting in line while I spoke to the cashier at the grocery store. A deep, abiding joy returned to my life as I shared my faith, hope, and zest for living.

ROAD MAP TO JOY

I was reminded of this truth again when standing at the shores of the Dead Sea. Everyone asks before they wade into the Dead Sea, "Can I really float?" Yes, yes, you can! Deadweight becomes light and buoyant in the sea. With a salinity of over 34 percent, the Dead Sea is one of the saltiest bodies of water in the world. It is also one of the most popular places for resorts. These salt waters have great healing benefits. The shoreline is crusted over with salt—it's even in the air and dries on your skin!

Just as the salt of the Dead Sea brings healing and restoration, our lives are meant to bring healing, hope, and truth to a hurting world. We are called to preserve what is good and reflect God's love in a way that refreshes and revives those around us.

Scripture
"Salt is good, but if the salt has lost its saltiness, how will you make it salty again? Have salt in yourselves, and be at peace with one another" (Mark 9:50, ESV).

Prayer

Dear Lord, I long to be a savory reflection of You that will cause those around me to thirst for You and Your kingdom. Restore my saltiness as I read Your Word and share my faith. Give me the courage and grace to speak up about salvation and Your work on the cross.

Activation

What's your salt level? It's important. I learned the hard way to watch my physical and spiritual sodium intake regularly. Death by low salt is miserable. I refuse to go down that pathway again. I know well that I have freely received salvation, and I freely long to pay it forward. Do you taste salty to the world? Make a goal of sharing your faith once a week, and keep tabs on your salt level regularly.

Further Study

Colossians 4:6, Luke 14:34–35, and 2 Peter 2:20–23

Some journeys take us far from home. Some adventures lead us to our destiny.

—THE CHRONICLES OF NARNIA: THE LION, THE WITCH AND THE WARDROBE

41

Dark and Sweet

The shy young Brazilian
maid smiles at me from
across the large, empty

room as she pours dark
and sweet morning coffee
into my clean, white cup.

The two of us are alone in
a big family kitchen,
stumbling over each other

in silence. Like an obedient
child, she waits to serve the
breakfast I do not want. I am

hungry to know her name,
about her family, her hometown.
Yearning to say more than,

"*Obrigado*," I repeat it over
and over. The maid knows me
from movies, TV, social media.

I know her from grade school
geography. She considers me
rich and fat, as she smiles and

pours another steaming stream
of dark and sweet liquid into my
empty, now coffee-stained cup.

—Belo Horizonte, Brazil

I wrote the following poem in the home of dear Brazilian friends. It is typical for Brazilians to employ several maids. I awoke before everyone and the maid was waiting in the kitchen to serve me. My Portuguese was all but nil, but I had such a yearning to communicate with her. Though she was attentive and sweet, she seemed unsure around foreigners like me. After breakfast I retreated to the porch with my journal and pen and began to write.

ROAD MAP TO JOY

Travel is one of the best remedies for racial misunderstandings. It is a bridge of wide-eyed awakening that breaks down the walls of preconceived prejudices that are born and flourish because of ignorance and/or apathy. One of life's joys is building friendships with many ethnic groups and learning from the beauty and wisdom of their traditions and customs.

Scripture
"From one man he made all nations, that they should inhabit the whole earth; and he marked out their appointed time in history and the boundaries of their lands" (Acts 17:26).

Prayer
Dear Lord, I recognize that You have created all humankind in Your beautiful image. I honor Your sovereignty over all nations. Help me recognize and seize opportunities to make lasting friendships with people who are different from me.

Activation
The Bible addresses discrimination among ethnic groups and races. It equips us with compassion and understanding to break all the dividing walls separating us. The best way to grow in unity is knowing what the Word of God says about how to recognize, love, and respect each other's sameness and differences. Find and meditate on these verses. Be prepared to joyfully embrace people you encounter on your journey from differing countries and backgrounds.

Further Study
Deuteronomy 32:7–8, Genesis 3:20, and Romans 5:12–19

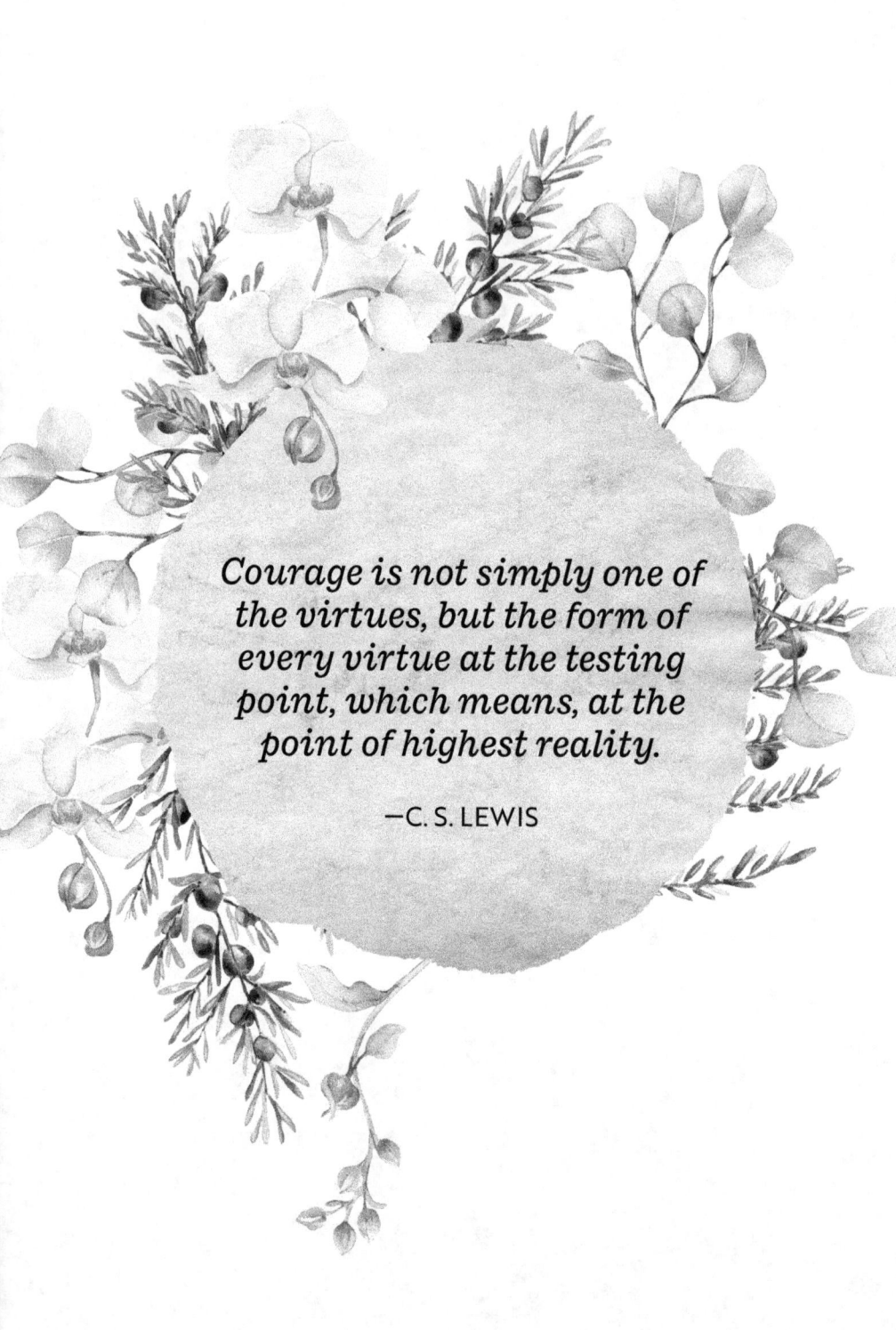

Courage is not simply one of the virtues, but the form of every virtue at the testing point, which means, at the point of highest reality.

—C. S. LEWIS

42

Culture Versus Content

In our daughter's early childhood Wayne took us on a driving tour through New England during the peak of autumn color. I recollect it as one of our most memorable vacations. We brought along Peter Marshall's book about early America, *The Light and the Glory*,[20] reading parts of it aloud as we traveled to important historical points along the way. The book, the sites, and the journey deepened our American patriotism. In some cases it righted our wrong thinking about our country's history.

Almost daily I feel the American culture pulling against my lifestyle as a Christian. Cancel and woke culture still threatens commonsense living, although lately, its grip seems to be loosening. Apathy to God and authority reigns. It is everywhere. I see it in the glaring lights of Hollywood, media, or politics and the people around me who worship wealth and easy living with their money, time, and interest.

Many don't care a whit about the covenant of marriage. Some never make promises to stay together for life. Every day, somewhere in our country, a battle rages for the sanctity of marriage, family, and life itself. The voices are so loud, and at times, it seems they drown out the foundational truths of our society.

The media is another cultural force pulling against my identity as a believer. Many journalists and writers today lean liberal in their views. Some maintain only a nominal connection to their church, while others are agnostic or atheistic. I agree that these are private choices in life, but they influence what the media produces. Television and movies elevate the triumph of the human spirit, free from the provision of God, and free from responsibility to each other. There is a strong pull away from God, the purity of marriage, and the rightness of family because of the media.

Although the movie *Love Story* is practically ancient now, it introduced a mindset that continues to be repeated through the media: "Love means never having to say you're sorry."[21] That is the most ridiculous thing I have ever heard. But Hollywood keeps the theme going with many sister spin-offs. To the believer, love is not the helpless pawn of feeling.

For love to live in beauty and truth, it means saying, "I am sorry," over and over and over.

Forgiveness is the most loving attitude toward a loved one.

Everyone makes mistakes, but Hollywood continues to perpetuate the idea that it is OK to let love blot out mistakes without words of repentance or taking responsibility. If you hurt someone you love, it is right to admit the mistake and say you are sorry. I even like to take it a step further by adding, "Will you please forgive me?" Words are powerful tools to bring healing.

Some people say the biggest culprit is Americans' craving for materialism. Some say this is our god. But based on my limited travel and cross-cultural experiences, I would say that materialism is not America's number one enemy keeping her from God and reaching out to others in love.

I believe it is isolationism. The root of isolationism is apathy–caring only about that which pertains to me or my family. "To hell with the rest of it" seems to be the mantra of American life. "I am going to take care of me and mine."

It is so rare to find people who are not holed up in their private, beautiful kingdoms (homes), who are not hell-bent on fulfilling their dreams to acquire better houses and cars or more time for leisure and pleasure, and who are instead genuinely concerned about pleasing God and reaching a hurting world.

American culture worships money and fame too much when it is contentment for which we yearn. We have grown apathetic to our God and our neighbors, yet we long for deep satisfaction. The pot of gold at the end of the rainbow won't buy contentment.

The kind of contentment that American culture provides is elusive and temporary. Our culture is abstract, although it feels concrete, surging against us in mighty waves of influence. Our choices are concrete, although they feel abstract, against the tide of humanism that engulfs us.

> There are absolutes, and those absolutes anchor us against the battering waves of a tumultuous society.

From the anchor of biblical truth, we are invited to make our choices. We create the contentment in our lives through those choices.

On the same autumn trip to New England, I wrote a poem about what it feels like to make choices hopefully and prayerfully with eternal content in mind—content contrary to my culture—yet that leads to my contentment. In fact, it leads to much more contentment and eternal life itself.

PILGRIM

Stark against society's
post-modern moving,
I pass as an ancient Bedouin,
nomad upon the desert.
Archaic curiosity
laughingstock,
a pilgrim wanderer
in search of higher ground,
not more.
Impassioned with a flaming heart
and light feet, I am
a pioneer who will not gather.
Shunned by the bleeding elite,
the tolerant intolerant,
the jealous,
the almost persuaded.
I count the spurn
privilege for joy's hope
set before me
to travel unhindered
unencumbered
upward
homeward bound.

ROAD MAP TO JOY

How do we find and keep contentment? How does our culture and all that entails—fables, forms, folklore, family, and fait—influence contentment?

The secrets of contentment are locked within our choices, which transcend the content of our culture. But we must make sure there is *eternal* content in our choices. There is a plumb line from which we measure all things in life, and it is rooted in eternity.

Scripture
"Pray also for me, that whenever I speak, words will be given to me so that I will fearlessly make known the mysteries of the gospel" (Eph. 6:19).

Prayer
Dear Lord, I need the help of the Holy Spirit to stand up for Jesus in the world today. Fill me with Your wisdom and boldness to know what to say, to whom, and when.

Activation
Speaking the truth with courage is daunting in our current cancel-culture society. Boldness is necessary, but perfect timing to make an impact is also important. Make it a habit to ask the Lord to give you a sensitivity to know with whom you should drop a few seeds of eternal hope each day. Breaking through to say the right words will fill your heart with joy.

Further Study
Ephesians 6:19, 1 Chronicles 28:20, and Joshua 1:9

> The very nature of Joy makes nonsense of our common distinction between having and wanting.
>
> —C. S. LEWIS

43

The Flood

Yesterday's burdens weighed you down,
too heavy for the long road as they
gathered in the corners of your

heart. Let the blueness of that wound you
bear today become a scouring tide; let
it rise and wash away winter's broken,

brown debris. Let the tears flow,
let the shock, anger, and resentment,
float to the top of the flood and let the

cleansing waters wash it back—out to the
vastness of the sea. Let suffering scrub
down deep. Let hope soak below your skin,

let it fill your nails as you scratch and climb
up out of the muddy deluge. Stretch out on
the Rock called Refuge, and let the sun dry your

face down to the bones of your heart. Breathe.
Expose your wounds and bruises to the sea air.
Count your fingers and toes in eternal light, and

see what's left—nothing but living joy and
gladness as clean and clear as glass pouring from
the water above called heaven.

ROAD MAP TO JOY

I wrote this poem after the devastating hurricanes and flooding in the southern states of the United States. It has remained applicable and a comfort to me in the aftermath of other natural disasters in the states and around the world. There have been too many with too much heartache. Amid this there are always the heroes of these devastations who rescue and risk their lives to save others. Alongside the loss and grief reside the comeback stories of the survivors who experienced the death of family, friends, and worldly goods yet press on to rebuild their lives with hope and renewal. Thank God for those who rise above the catastrophes with eternal hope. Light and joy can be regained by finding the eternal stream of God's grace while expressing gratitude and praise through it all. This is the pathway to joy amid loss and suffering.

Scripture
"Have mercy on me, my God, have mercy on me, for in you I take refuge. I will take refuge in the shadow of your wings until the disaster has passed" (Ps. 57:1–2).

Prayer
Dear Lord, I thank You that Your Word promises that You are a very present help in trouble. I ask for immediate protection and saving grace to find safety and help.

Activation
Whether you or a family member is facing a natural catastrophic event or the aftermath, prayer is essential. It is a powerful force for overcoming with strength, hope, and courage in difficult times. Cry out to God for salvation and help like never before. You will be amazed and filled with joy to witness His answers of provision and help.

Further Study
Proverbs 3:25–36, Psalm 46:1–2, and 2 Corinthians 4:9

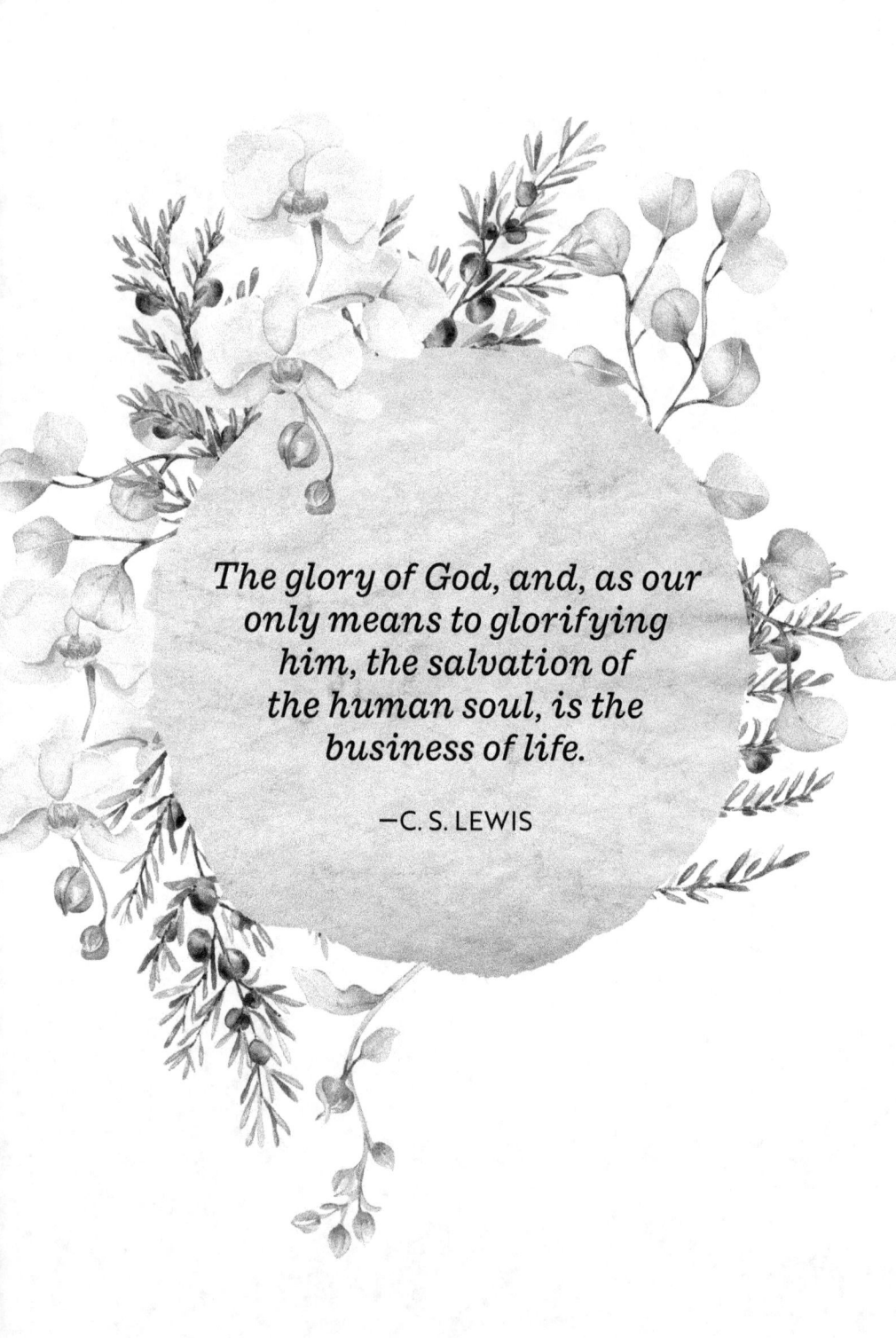

The glory of God, and, as our only means to glorifying him, the salvation of the human soul, is the business of life.

—C. S. LEWIS

The Right to Speak

Sometimes you must engage in a dozen or more casual conversations before you earn the right to speak into someone's life. It is worth it!

There is a proper order for leaders as well as laypeople to offer a significant hand in bringing healing to the hurting and making disciples. There is so much shock and disappointment around us, and each person is dealing with their own.

That does not disqualify us as decent human beings to continue to reach out to those around us. It doesn't even have to be someone you know; it can be the person standing in line next to you at Target. The key is to be alert to the desperately hurting and ready to make a connection. And often, this connection is a casual meeting with nothing profound other than coffee. It may happen a dozen or more times before a real connection is developed, and it is the pathway to true freedom.

Earning the right to speak into other people's lives is an ongoing challenge. When my daughter was about twelve years old, she asked me why I didn't hang out in her bedroom and just talk to her. She named mothers we both knew that did this regularly with their children. As I reflected upon that conversation, I became pierced to the heart. I recall that I had spent most of my time correcting her actions, giving her ultimatums, or barking out rights and wrongs. I had forgotten that the foundation of tenderness was developing her trust and confidence before endeavoring to mold her into a God-fearing, decent human.

I needed that rebuke and tried to change. Because I invested little into our relationship and more into discipline, I was losing the right to be heard and taken seriously.

Conversely, in my places of employment or when I lived in other countries, I consciously endeavored to express care and empathy toward colleagues or neighbors before dropping the seeds of the gospel. I found this to be effective. Often those around me would initiate conversations about wanting prayer or more assurance about life or death.

There are millions hurting and in need of truth and healing living in the darkness. Only a few cross my path daily, but timing is always key.

It is worth the patience to let love and trust grow before offering the pearl of great price.

Again and again, earning the right to speak is worth the investment.

ROAD MAP TO JOY

Someone is waiting for your genuine connection—completely unaware that your pocket holds consolation, cheer, and counsel, should there arise the need. In your pocket resides the keys to eternal life, peace, joy, reconciliation, and true hope for a wonderful future. Here is a simple outline to guide you through the steps of making a lasting connection.

Connect—Take the Initiative
> However, the spiritual is not first, but the natural, then afterward the spiritual.
> —1 Corinthians 15:46, NKJV

Console—Listen Without Judgment or Advice, Empathize
> Casting all your anxieties on him, because he cares for you.
> —1 Peter 5:7, ESV

Cheer—Encourage and Build Up

You cannot encourage a friend or acquaintance fully until you first connect and console. These prepare the heart to receive solace.

> Therefore encourage one another and build one another up, just as you are doing.
> —1 Thessalonians 5:11, ESV

Counsel—Be Sincere

Unsolicited or unearned counsel is rarely effective.
> But the wisdom from above is first pure, then peaceable, gentle, open to reason, full of mercy and good fruits, impartial and sincere.
> —James 3:17, ESV

Scripture

"So we fix our eyes not on what is seen, but on what is unseen, since what is seen is temporary, but what is unseen is eternal" (2 Cor. 4:18).

Prayer

Dear Lord, help me realize that trust to share the gospel is often earned. Help me remember as I develop friendships that spiritual truths are spiritually discerned. Let my love for others grow, and show me when and what to share as I learn to genuinely care for and love those around me.

Activation

Earning the right to speak is worth the investment. The key is loving your neighbor, or those in your pathway, as yourself. This love and servanthood lead to eternal conversations. Ask God for ways to love, serve, and, when the time is right, share.

Further Study

1 Corinthians 2:14, 1 Corinthians 15:45, and Romans 6:6

Gratefulness unlocks life; graciousness unlocks people.

45

You Sobered Your Soul

> Love is not an affectionate feeling, but a steady wish for the loved person's ultimate good as far as it can be obtained.
> —C. S. Lewis

During the fat of summer,
your thin hands
embraced the razor cold
of winter. Your heart

rejected lethargy in that
joyful day of ease.
You sobered your soul
to tailor family hats,

mittens, and coats.
I watched you dip them
in blood
and soak them in tears.

You gathered oil and
wheat and wine
and dug a cave for
eternity

in the fragile, volatile
state of abundance.
When others played
in the shallow light

of summer, you sobered
your soul. At the first
drop of rain,
we hunkered down

in that dark cellar of faith.
You smiled when the wind
blew the candles out, and
the old, rickety wooden table

jiggled as we wrote our
lessons in the light of eternity.
You made sure our feet did
not slip. You squeezed the

color from vegetables and
painted a canvas of possibility;
and when we ate the last bite
of soup, I saw you bow

your knee to one who is
greater. You warred for my life
and freed my feet and hands
to jump over a wall with

ease, to stop an enemy in
his tracks, to tie the shoe of
a child, to recognize a thirsty
soul, and to understand

when a silver world begins
to tarnish. You taught me
how to cope with clay feet
and golden dreams

when you took away my
measuring rod. For this,
you are wise and good,
you are called Mother.

ROAD MAP TO JOY

In Jerusalem, a very ancient city filled with stone, everywhere you look, you will find flowers cracking through rocks. Its picturesque metaphor deeply encourages my life journey. I also love the contrast between the soft flower that breaks the hard stone because of the power of life and beauty within it.

That's what mothers teach their children—to be both hard and soft, hard on selfishness and self-absorption, hard on learning discipline and strong work ethics, yet soft on developing compassion for others and love for God, family, and neighbors. The examples are limitless. Mom, thanks for teaching me to be both hard and soft. I am so grateful for your example of faith and prayer, for loving me when I was rebellious and unlovable, and for never giving up when life was hard! Your steadiness has helped me in countless ways in my life. I wrote this poem for Mother's Day and never tire of the words that honor motherhood and the deep love mothers develop for their children and families.

Scripture
"She is clothed with strength and dignity; she can laugh at the days to come" (Prov. 31:25).

Prayer

Dear Lord, thank You for my mother. I chose to honor her and forgive the ways that she has failed me. I bless her memory. Help me be a better parent in Your strength and wisdom. If motherhood has been denied to me for some reason, show me the ways that I can connect to others with the maternal treasures of love, generosity, and kindness.

Activation

We find so much to treasure in the examples of a loving mother. There is wisdom, selflessness, frugality, and strength beyond measure. Perhaps your mother fits this description, or maybe not. Take time to honor her. If your experience is the opposite, you have the power to change the narrative in your family for the generations that follow by being that mother—not perfect, rather unconditionally loving and generous with God's help.

Further Study

Isaiah 66:13, Luke 11:13, and John 15:13

46

Two Stories Becoming One

For many years, when Wayne put Julia to bed, he told her a bedtime story.

"Mama and Daddy got married and couldn't have children. We knew God had a wonderful plan, though. We prayed for God to send us a very special child chosen by Him. So, God looked *all* over the world (with animated hand gestures but then pointing dramatically to Julia), and *He chose you*." This made Julia giggle with delight.

Julia loved the story and asked us to tell her over and over when she was little. Her adoption day created a unique opportunity because she celebrated two birthdays—the day she was born in Guatemala and the day we brought her home. The latter we called her "happy day." Growing up, she felt privileged to have two days, not just one.

Wayne and I tried to make her experience filled with joy and adventure.

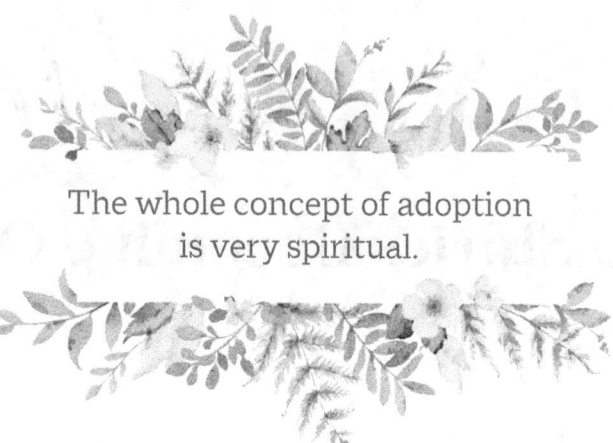

The whole concept of adoption is very spiritual.

We are all adopted children, rescued from darkness and born into God's kingdom of light.

In Guatemala another story played out that brought Julia to us. Estella, Julia's birth mother, was born in San Marcos, a Guatemalan city bordering Mexico. Eighteen children were born to Estella's mother—only ten lived. Four children died at birth and four later. Estella was the seventh of ten. Her father, a poor farmer, died when she was eleven.

Estella's mother sent her to Guatemala City to live and work for a family. She never returned home and worked as a maid in various places. She conceived a son and later met and married Julia's father, Carlos.

Together, Carlos and Estella had another son and two girls. Their life was very difficult. They lived with Carlos' family, but they did not like Estella and treated her very badly, telling lies about her. When she became pregnant with Julia, Carlos' mother told him the baby was not his. Carlos believed this story, but Julia was his child. He threatened Estella to try to persuade her not to have the baby. She feared for her life while pregnant with Julia—it was the hardest season she had ever faced.

She fled, saved the baby, and didn't know what to do but give her up for adoption. She got in touch with a lawyer.

We knew nothing about this, but we had prayed fervently for the right child to come to us. Then, a lawyer called Shady Grove Church to ask if anyone was interested in adopting a baby.

We contacted the lawyer immediately, and then one day he called to say that a girl had been born to Estella. He said, "I have her birth certificate in front of me. What do you want to name her?" Well, we had prayed and already knew her name: Julia Elizabeth.

It took another six months before all the red tape of adoption was clear. We flew to Guatemala City and brought her home.

After hearing Estella's story, we understood more than ever that Julia's life had been "snatched out of the mouth of a lion." These are the very words God put in my heart as we prayed for a breakthrough in the months waiting for Julia to become ours.

Estella felt her and Julia's lives were in jeopardy. And although it was hard, it was a very loving thing for Estella to do, to give Julia up for adoption. She could have aborted her. God had other plans for our Julia.

Ten years ago Estella heard the gospel and repented of her sins. She became a true believer. She prayed to meet Julia one time in her life. And God answered that prayer.

Carlos is still living. Estella rarely sees him. She does not think that he knows that Julia was born. That is the sad part of the story.

It is so wonderful to see how God was at work, blending two stories and bringing people together. He is always bringing lives together to love and to reflect His glory.

When Julia turned twenty-one, she asked to meet her birth mother in person. Wayne contacted the lawyer, and through an amazing miracle, he found Estella and arranged a meeting. Estella, and Julia's eleven siblings, took several buses to meet us. When they met for the first time, they embraced as Estella cried and buried her head in Julia's shoulder. It was so sweet—everyone cried.

We stayed at the restaurant for nearly four hours just visiting, catching up, and discovering facts about each other's lives, having lived in different countries for twenty-one years.

The most important thing we discovered was that Julia's mom had become a true believer ten years prior, ever since she prayed and prayed for the opportunity to see Julia again.

ROAD MAP TO JOY

Wayne and I completed infertility testing with no answers. We prayed and believed God placed joy and faith in our hearts to adopt and led us to the right baby. This is a very personal choice, but if you are struggling with infertility or the path toward adoption, I hope you are encouraged by our story.

Scripture
"I prayed for this child, and the Lord has granted me what I asked of him" (1 Sam. 1:27).

Prayer
Dear Lord, thank You for the beautiful love for Your children, which is reflected in adoption. I ask for peace and guidance as I begin this process. Calm my fears and lead me to make the right choices. I believe You long to bless our family with a child to love.

Activation
The New Testament states that true religion is caring for orphans and widows. This is a great passage to remember if you are considering adoption. Although it can be a stressful process, accepting someone else's child is a beautiful picture of God's unconditional love.

Further Study
1 John 5:15, Matthew 7:7, and Psalm 118:5

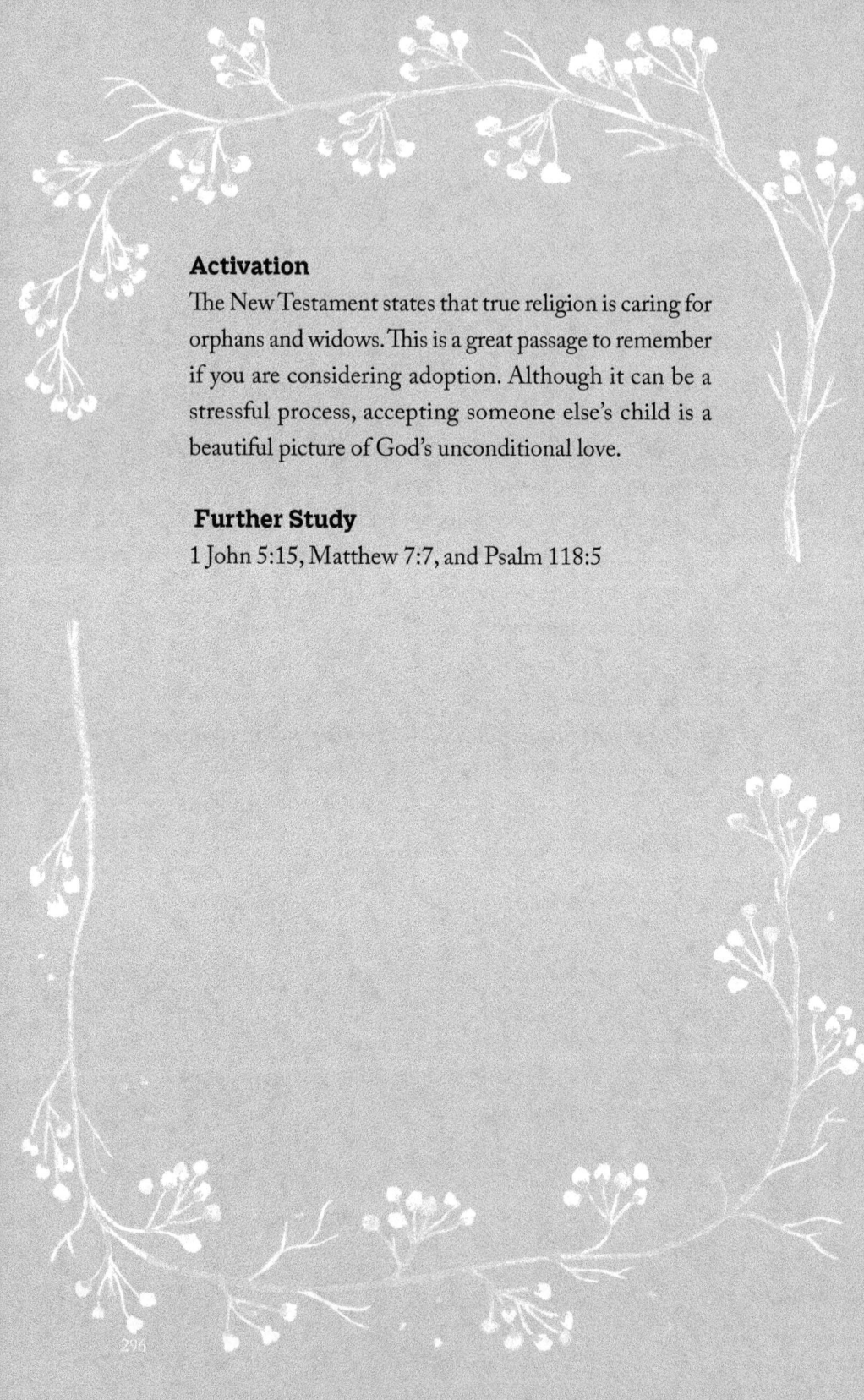

*Heaven is not a state of mind.
Heaven is reality itself.*

—C. S. LEWIS

47

Skull Hill

In heaven, Skull Hill
will never be a faint
memory, rather a mountain
we climb daily. The practice
of devotion
will continue, learned from
our earthly courses and lessons
in overcoming in victory. In
Paradise,

we can stop the
climb,

but we won't desire that.

The journey to the cross is
too familiar in heart
and the garden, dewy and rose-scented,
at the top,
too sweet and fragrant and
peaceful for lingering.

Calvary will never be a foggy
dream but a present truth—
a reality
that puts the value in the gates
of precious stones,
gleam in the golden
streets, sparkle in
Crystal River, and the meaning

in the crown
I will relinquish
when I touch His scars.

ROAD MAP TO JOY

Prayer and worship are foundational in my life. In Matthew 10:39 Jesus tells the disciples, "Whoever finds their life will lose it, and whoever loses their life for my sake will find it." Thousands of years later, we too follow in the footsteps of Jesus, who ascended Skull Hill, or Calvary, in obedience to the Father. The Son willingly, not without great struggle, ascended the mountain of death in Jerusalem to indeed conquer the ultimate enemy.

During my quiet time with Jesus, I plan and prepare spiritually for the day, living out this truth. Each day brings surprises, but this practice has proven to be my strength. Often, sometimes hour by hour, I may be called upon to do, say, and think things that are contrary to laying my life down for Christ or others. The battle is easier if it is won in the morning before I leave. Although I am called a disciple, honestly, I am undisciplined and in need of a swift kick every now and then. My story is not different from yours.

One morning something shifted. As I pondered climbing Calvary each day to pray, prepare, and offer petition and thanksgiving, my recollections were fragrant, not bitter. Reaching the top of the hill or, if you will, the cross, I was met by sweetness and an intimate relationship full of love and compassion.

Because I learned to love my climb to Calvary to worship and surrender each day, I think of what heaven will be like. Jesus promised to wipe our tears away and remove all pain and suffering. We are admonished on this earth when we partake of the Lord's Supper to remember the Lord in His death. Does that mean its memory will vanish with the coming of the new heaven and earth? I can't imagine, because it has become the sweetest place on earth to me. I feel I will still long for it in heaven.

Scripture
"For the past troubles will be forgotten and hidden from my eyes. See, I will create new heavens and a new earth. The former things will not be remembered, nor will they come to mind" (Isa. 65:16–17).

Prayer
Dear Lord, thank You for the earth's beauty and the wonderful memories I've lived here. As I anticipate heaven, I thank You for taking away my suffering and drying my

tears as You promised. You created me in a certain way, and it thrills me that we will continue in relationship in heaven without sin, suffering, or sorrowful memory.

Activation

Could it be that all of earth's sorrows will be forgotten, but some of our best memories will remain? By the blood of Jesus, they will be washed, redeemed, and purified but not obliterated. I imagine we may remember many precious moments with the people we love from our time on earth. One of my favorite memories to keep will be my intimate moments with the Lord climbing Calvary—in a sense losing my life but finding only sweet release, surrender, and joy. It has become a place of both brokenness and strength. My best place and space to linger. I want to retain its memory in heaven. As you anticipate a new eternal place to live someday, what dear memories would you like to take with you?

Further Study

Exodus 34:6, Job 11:16, and Isaiah 45:23

> *God cannot give us happiness and peace apart from Himself, because it is not there.*
>
> —C. S. LEWIS

48

The Pink Bomb Shelter

A dank, moldy smell rose as I descended the dark stairwell of the bomb shelter. I pulled my scarf tighter around my face and nose as the air grew colder and mustier.

I found the belly of the underground refuge filled with flickering candles, laughter, Christmas goodies, and faces from many countries: Germany, Switzerland, Argentina, Romania, the United States, Israel, England, and Russia. We were all volunteers on Kibbutz Einat, located outside of Tel Aviv, Israel. And we were very far from home on an important evening of the year.

Our volunteer group from Texas originally consisted of thirty young people the summer before, a few of us staying for the rest of the year. It was a marvelous opportunity. We worked during the day, studied Hebrew at night, and had many chances to develop friendships with the local Jewish and Arab Israelis and a myriad of volunteers from various nations.

Our group gained favor with the kibbutz leaders. They gave us a bomb shelter of our own to use for worship, prayer, Bible studies, meetings, and parties. They also gave us paint to brighten it up. We slathered the walls with pink!

In the summer it was a sweet escape from the heat of the day. We gathered almost daily to have times of worship and prayer together. But we used it less when there were just a handful of us left to forge the rest of the year alone.

It was the perfect place for a Christmas Eve party for all the volunteers. The American group hosted the event. The kibbutz donated food, some volunteers spending the day in the kitchen creating special sweets from home—tortes, Danishes, and apple strudel. I made chocolate chip cookies, which none of the foreign volunteers had tasted. They were a big hit!

It was already dark when we gathered in the bomb shelter for our festivities. We dove into the food, telling jokes and stories. At the close of the evening, a volunteer started singing "Silent Night" in German. Then we joined her in our own languages. We sang several Christmas carols familiar to all of us, each in his mother tongue. The beautiful music vibrated the walls of the shelter. It was the grandest place on earth that night and couldn't have been more beautiful or special if it had been in the most elegant hotel in the world.

There was a deep sense of unity and peace as we remembered the baby born in Bethlehem. Tears filled my eyes as the music lifted our spirits and sent us soaring on an evening that could have been the loneliest of the year for all of us so far away from home.

That moment is branded onto my heart and gave me a little taste of what it might be like in heaven when every nation, tongue, and tribe comes before the throne of God to give Him praise—when every knee will bow to proclaim Jesus as Lord and thank Him for coming to earth, for dying, for giving new life.

The evening ended. To my utter amazement, when I ascended the stairs, I found a group of Israeli kibbutz members standing outside the door, listening to our music. I had no idea how long they had been listening in the cold, but none of them seemed to mind.

One young man pulled me aside and said, "This bomb shelter has been a place of war, but you have made it a place of peace."

I have never forgotten those words. Every time war comes to Israel, as the bombs are flying and people are fleeing for shelter in their refuges, I think of the glow of our pink bomb shelter. I remember all the prayers said in that place for reconciliation between Arabs and Jews, for peace in Jerusalem, for the eyes of Israel and the whole world to be opened to their Messiah.

Every Christmas and Hanukkah season, I remember that evening, knowing I had a little taste of "peace on earth, goodwill toward men." It happened in a pink bomb shelter—the most unlikely place.

And I want more.

ROAD MAP TO JOY

"The Pink Bomb Shelter" was written during my second year in Israel while I was living on Kibbutz Einat. Since then a number of years have passed, and since then the land of milk and honey has endured a heinous war of another kind, the October 7, 2023 massacre. Since, my husband and I returned to Israel to hear the stories of survivors, to weep with them in their mourning, and to rejoice with their miracles as well.

While there, we were eating at a seafood restaurant along the beaches in Tel Aviv when sirens began to blast. Everyone stood and walked to the designated shelter nearby. That event became my first real-time experience with running for protection from the threat of a flying rocket. I remembered the pink bomb shelter of my kibbutz days and all the prayers in that place. I thank God for holy protection and that He keeps His promise to protect and love His people, the Jews. I also wondered if my own country could experience war like this someday.

Scripture
"Indeed, he who watches over Israel will neither slumber nor sleep. The Lord watches over you—the Lord is your shade at your right hand; the sun will not harm you by day, nor the moon by night" (Ps. 121:4–6).

Prayer
Dear Lord, I remember Your promise to protect me when the world overwhelms me. I entrust my life to Your safety and lovingkindness.

Activation
As a Christian, I am so grateful for the Jewish people who have given the world so much—the Bible; Jesus; the Ten Commandments, which have been a code of conduct for the entire world; the Holy Land; and the blessing of the Jewish people themselves. Genesis 12:3 tells us that the Jews are called by God to be a blessing to the entire world. This has proved to be true.

The same passage in Genesis instructs all nations to bless the Jewish people; that whoever does will, in turn, be blessed, and whoever refuses will be cursed. I believe these words and live my life accordingly. Take a personal account of your thoughts and actions concerning the Jewish people. If you find anti-Semitism hiding there, ask God to forgive you and to teach you to love and embrace His people. As you read the Bible, notice God's great love for Israel. The Christian story is rooted within God's love story with Israel, the Jewish people of promise.

Further Study
Psalm 121:2, Psalm 121, and Psalm 90

Recommended Reading
Our Hands Are Stained with Blood: The Tragic Story of the Church and the Jewish People by Michael L. Brown, *Restoring the Jewishness of the Gospel: A Message for Christians* by David Stern, *What Does the Bible Really Say About the Land?* by Asher Intrater, and *Who Ate Lunch with Abraham?: A Study of the Appearances of God in the Form of a Man in the Hebrew Scriptures* by Asher Intrater

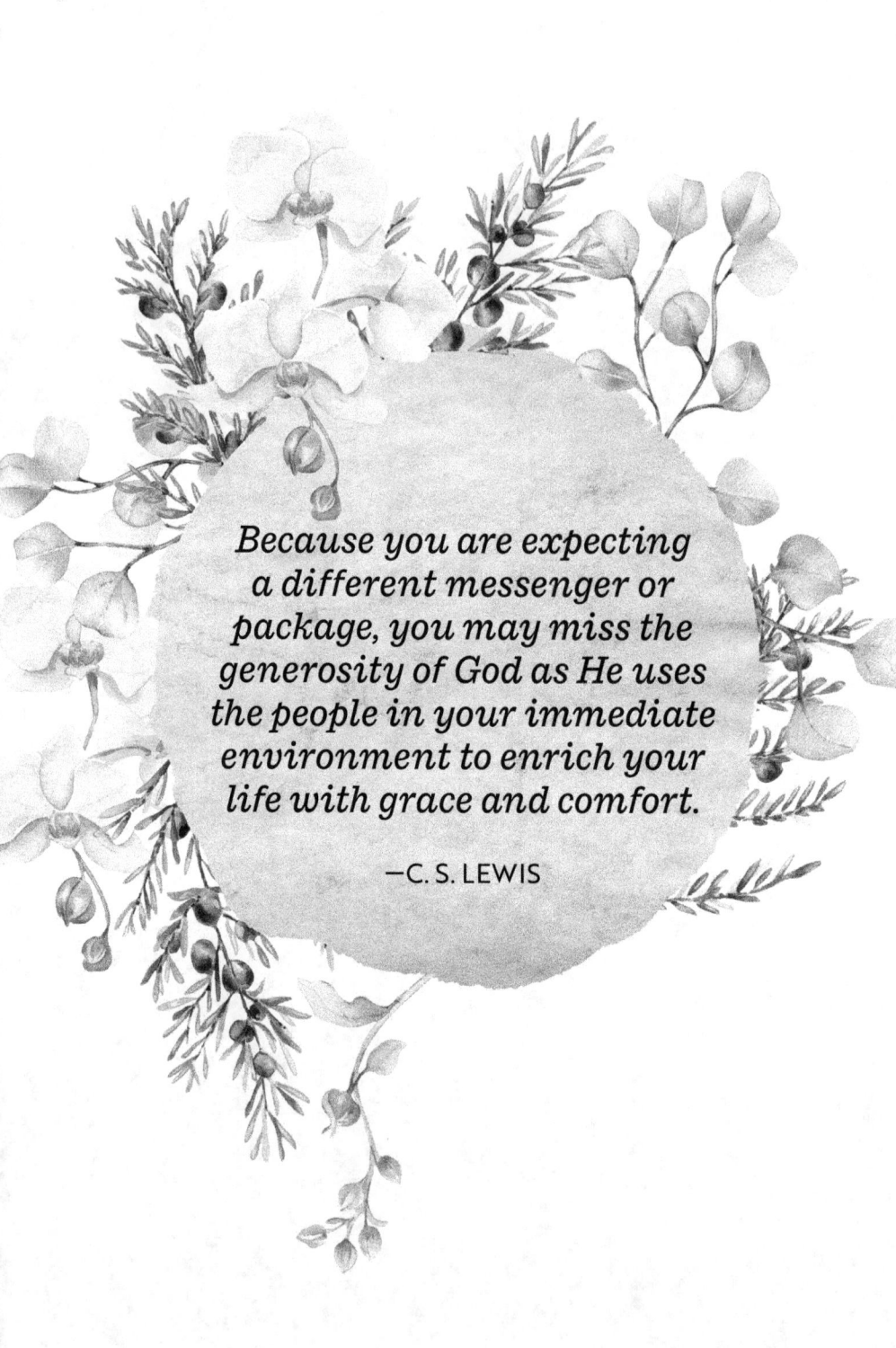

Because you are expecting a different messenger or package, you may miss the generosity of God as He uses the people in your immediate environment to enrich your life with grace and comfort.

—C. S. LEWIS

49

To Begin Again

There are better things ahead than any we leave behind.
—C. S. Lewis

I have tasted wine in Bordeaux, picked lavender from a sunlit purple field, and awoken slowly from long, luxurious summer naps in French villas. I've lifted crystal flutes filled with white bubble elixir in countryside *maisons de Champagne* and indulged in leisurely three-course meals in outdoor cafes perched next to ancient castles and rolling green hills.

I have sat with French families and friends around a big, round family table filled with food and wine and relished conversations of depth, mind, and heart. And there, serendipitously, I discovered the very root of exquisite cuisine that derives from the depth of the French heart and mind.

There I met two lively older French women who had dedicated their lives to prayer and the reconciliation of people groups throughout the world. They extended to me—a pampered, self-centered American—long, loving arms of hospitality and unconditional acceptance. So long, they reached into the deepest wound of me to love, heal, and mend.

It was there that I fell in love—not with France but with the God of the French. It was then that I fell on bent knee with sobbing and contrition, pleading for forgiveness for my arrogance against the French and all nations. It was there that I rose, after traveling the world for twenty-five years, to begin again.

ROAD MAP TO JOY

When Wayne and I travel to other countries, connecting with leaders and members of other churches, my favorite people to meet are the stalwart people of faithful prayer. They are the heroes of faith who see things in the Spirit realm and do nothing but the serious work of intercession on bended knees. And they don't give up! Wars have been stopped, and nations changed by these humble servants. Heaven has a special reward for these heroes.

Little did I know God saw some threads of prejudice in my heart against other ethnicities. If someone would have asked me, I would have exclaimed, "No, not me!" I do not know where it came from, but He faithfully revealed it! I would have continued in blind arrogance had those precious French ladies not come into our lives to influence us as friends and servants to make us more effective. I didn't fight it or defend my thoughts and actions. It brought humility, and I just received it and repented. Our relationship deeply changed my attitude toward others with various backgrounds.

Christ has given us the work of reconciliation. God loves the uniqueness of each nation. Each is important to Him with their special gifts, uniqueness, and beauty. That is why the book of Revelation reminds us that every tongue, tribe, and nation will gather before His throne in heaven one day. I long to love the nations as Christ did, doing all, even to the point of death, to reconcile them to Him in love.

Scripture
"All this is from God, who reconciled us to himself through Christ and gave us the ministry of reconciliation: that God was reconciling the world to himself in Christ, not counting people's sins against them. And he has committed to us the message of reconciliation" (2 Cor. 5:18–19).

Prayer
Dear Lord, bring me into acceptance, peace, and unity with diverse nations and ethnic groups. Help me seek justice for them with understanding and compassion. Bring healing where there has been prejudice and/or past conflicts and mistreatment.

Activation
I always considered myself to be free from prejudice until I was shown a dark part of my heart. I did not try to explain it away or justify it. I just received it and asked God to correct me and give me love instead of pride. I felt a thousand pounds fall from my shoulders. I carried a burden I did not know! Sincerely inquire of the Lord to show you if there is any people group or country you have ignorantly held at arm's length because of differences. The Lord will lead you into a lifestyle of reconciliation toward all nations and peoples. This is the love of Jesus.

Further Study
Romans 5:10–11, Ephesians 2:16–17, and 1 John 4:10

Recommended Reading
That They May Be One: A Brief Review of Church Restoration Movements and Their Connection to the Jewish People by Dan C. Juster, ThD; *Handbook for TJCII Intercessors* by Peter Hocken; and *What Christians Should Know About Reconciliation* by John Dawson

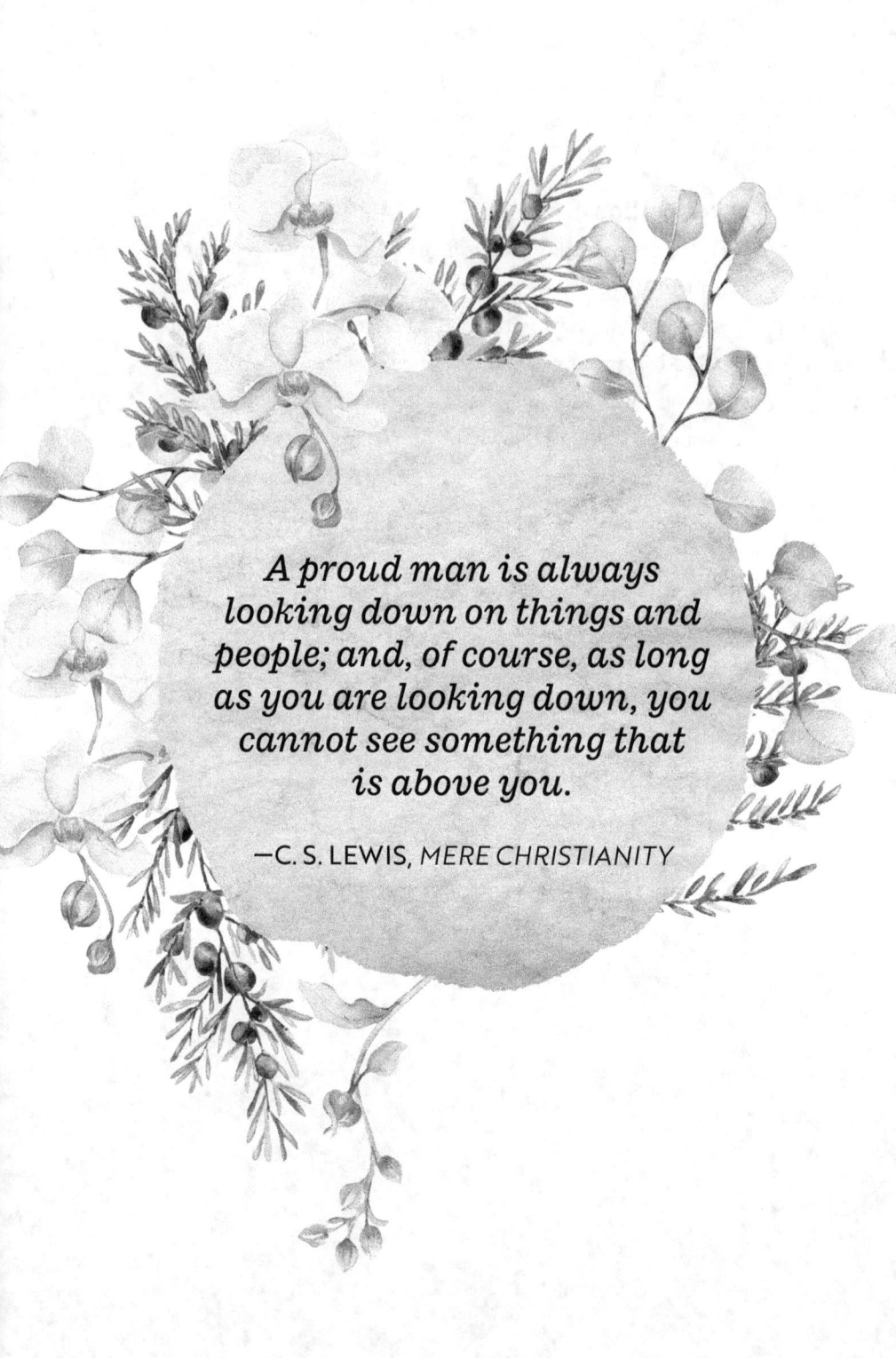

> *A proud man is always looking down on things and people; and, of course, as long as you are looking down, you cannot see something that is above you.*
>
> —C. S. LEWIS, *MERE CHRISTIANITY*

50

Angels, the Burning Ones

Away with tears and fears and troubles! United in wedlock with the eternal Godhead itself, our nature ascends into the Heaven of Heavens. So, it would be impious to call ourselves 'miserable.' On the contrary, Man is a creature whom the Angels—were they capable of envy— would envy. Let us lift up our hearts!
—C. S. Lewis

In my immediate world the season of fall brings a plethora of ideas and events to life. There is, of course, the bountiful splendor of harvest and the variegated colors of autumn, which are glorious and stand in their beauty.

The fall and winter holidays bring abundance, warm memories, light, focus, family and friends near, and an overwhelming flurry of activity. In these special days I pause, reflect, and joy in the mellow passing of days and unparalleled moments. I know these times will comfort my heart in leaner days unseen, unknown.

This is also the season of giving.

Many churches and nonprofit organizations present and host their annual missions' conferences or fundraisers during these months. It is a time of sacrifice, and there is a plethora of opportunities to give and bless others. While we are enjoying the fruits of abundance and harvest, we are at the same time giving to others. Opposite actions running on parallel tracks—giving and receiving.

These are not in conflict.

Recently we enjoyed the last Sunday of our own missionary conference. It was an amazing day filled with people from all over the world in the congregation. Everyone was ready and willing to worship and hear encouraging stories about missionaries taking the good news around the world.

It is something I had considered in the past, but a revelation about this season hit me harder than ever. Giving to missionaries or nonprofit organizations to advance the kingdom of God and reduce the suffering of humankind is their worthy projects, ministries, or outreaches.

The gifts we offer are about coming before a holy God and making a significant sacrifice to Him.

This is the best we should and can do considering His great gift to us—Jesus. The gift is a sacrifice to the Lord and Him alone. Indeed, it is set apart and holy.

The widow who gave two mites, or less than a penny, offered the most. It was all she had, and she is remembered forever for her sacrifice to the Lord. Oh, how she loved!

Mary broke open an alabaster jar and poured out the fragrance of death that became life, changing the atmosphere of her world. Some were deeply convicted and blessed, while others criticized her in the background. Her gift was too lavish, too costly, too over-the-top. It was the best she had, and her offering is recounted with conviction and faith. God loved her sacrifice, and Jesus received it graciously and openly.

Considering sacrifice, I have spent weeks meditating on Isaiah 6. I am moved to tears and action when I consider the seraphim's praise:

> In the year that King Uzziah died, I saw the Lord, high and exalted, seated on a throne; and the train of his robe filled the temple. Above him were seraphim, each with six wings: With two wings they covered their faces, with two they covered their feet, and with two they were flying. And they were calling to one another:
>
> "Holy, holy, holy is the Lord Almighty; the whole earth is full of his glory."
>
> At the sound of their voices the doorposts and thresholds shook, and the temple was filled with smoke.
>
> "Woe to me!" I cried. "I am ruined! For I am a man of unclean lips, and I live among a people of unclean lips, and my eyes have seen the King, the Lord Almighty."
>
> Then one of the seraphim flew to me with a live coal in his hand, which he had taken with tongs from the

altar. With it he touched my mouth and said, "See, this has touched your lips; your guilt is taken away and your sin atoned for."

Then I heard the voice of the Lord saying, "Whom shall I send? And who will go for us?"

And I said, "Here am I. Send me!"

—Isaiah 6:1–8

Seraphim (שְׂרָפִים) in Hebrew means the "burning ones." They burn with zeal and love for God, and this is their profound expression before Him and reflection of Him. Burning.

I am sure they are beautiful and maybe could fly to the moon with their magnificent, mighty, and strong wings. But when they are in the presence of a holy God, they use two wings to cover their faces and two wings to cover their feet in humility. Their remaining two wings are used to fly about and declare, "Holy, holy is the Lord God Almighty."

Those burning angels make a sacrifice to God.

Why? Because they know something about Him we don't—something we have yet to discover. They have glimpsed Him in purity and love as we have not. They have felt His awe and power and have known the expanse of His dominion and the depth of His ability to create light and dark, good and evil.

They are in awe. They are humbled. They *know* to sacrifice two-thirds of their resources—their wing power and flight ability—before the only one true God. It is a natural response because they have seen Him face-to-face. They use their gift of flight and their beauty—their wings—to blanket themselves in humility.

It is a sweet sacrifice to God.

Their feet are amazing too. They are the messengers of the Lord, going only where He leads them on divine missions. Still, they cover their feet with wings in humility. They make sacrifices before the King of kings.

> They use their best gifts to go low before God and change the atmosphere through their actions.

The seraphim's voices cry out, "Holy," and the doorposts and pillars of the Temple shake. Smoke arises.

Imagine that!

The men and women who hear and see this are changed—forever changed. They begin to repent of sin and beg for cleansing. Those who hear and see realize their actions do not equal their remarks or lip service.

The angels take hot coals from the altar to purge the uncleanness. And the only response from Isaiah the prophet was, "Send me!" He knew the rest of the world must see, hear, and experience what had been revealed in the presence of God.

In the duplicity of the season of giving and receiving, God pours out abundance that is revealed in our everyday world. He asks in return that we give all back to Him in holy sacrifice, which is our reasonable response.

I am taking a lesson from the seraphim—the burning ones—who know something about God I have yet to discover. A life of generous sacrifice is to live a life of exceeding joy.

ROAD MAP TO JOY

In today's culture the admonition or calling to a life of sacrifice is not popular. Teachings and sermons on overcoming hardship, suffering, or gaining the material blessing of God are more palatable. Scripture tells us that many are called but few are chosen. I have never fully understood this, nor do I pretend to know, but I wrote this essay years before my family left for the mission field in Odesa, Ukraine. God was preparing us for a life of sacrifice. We lived nine years abroad in four countries and experienced the best and worst of times. I count it all joy now, although there were some days when I wanted to bolt and live a different kind of life.

The seraphim, who see the form of the godhead daily in the courts of heaven, taught me just how important our sacrifices to God really are. They are not concerned with their achievements or position in the world materially, only worshipping God and crying out, "Holy, holy, holy." I think they say that three times over and over because in His presence there is nothing else to do. The road map to joy becomes evident through a daily lifestyle of obedience, which leads to sacrifice. Exuberant and boundless joy is the reward that overtakes the end of the journey.

Scripture
"Each of the four living creatures had six wings and was covered with eyes all around, even under its wings. Day and night they never stopped saying, 'Holy, holy, holy is the Lord God Almighty,' who was, and is, and is to come" (Rev. 4:8).

Prayer
Dear Lord, enable me to surrender my life ambitions and dreams to You alone. Direct me to become a light shining in darkness as a reflection of Your love and life that sets men free. Allow me to find the deepest joy in service to Your kingdom for Your glory alone.

Activation
Meditation on this verse became foundational in my own life of service and sacrifice:

Therefore, I urge you, brothers and sisters, in view of God's mercy, to offer your bodies as a living sacrifice, holy and pleasing to God—this is your true and proper worship.
—Romans 12:1

If you are considering a devout calling of service, meditate on and pray this verse often. It builds courage and strength as you activate these living words of faith. Also, seek counsel from mature believers whom you admire and who have gone before you in devoted steps of selfless love.

Further Study
Exodus 4:10–13, Acts 26:16–17, and Ephesians 3:8

*You will make known to me the way
of life; in Your presence is fullness
of joy; in Your right hand there are
pleasures forever.*

—PSALM 16:11, NASB

*We look away from the natural realm and
focus our attention and expectation onto
Jesus who birthed faith within us and who
leads us forward into faith's perfection.
His example is this: Because his heart
was focused on the joy of knowing that
you would be his, he endured the agony of
the cross and conquered its humiliation,
and now sits exalted at the right hand of
the throne of God!*

—HEBREWS 12:2, TPT

THE LIGHT OF JOY

Happiness is joy's
counterfeit and sorrow
its truest test. When

you finally perceive,
down deep, the price
and prize of redemption,

you are free to bend
life's bruises and victories
into the shape of over-

coming, everlasting joy.
Verbal, sacrificial praise
releases a fountain gate to

an ocean of exuberance
available to those that
bound beyond the

limitations of simple
gratefulness, that have
plunged into the amnesiac

depths of cleansing blood
and just can't stop saying,
thank You, thank You,
thank You!

JOY

Joy is something you swallow in big, lavish gulps, and something you exude—to give away—like perfumed ointment.

Endnotes

1 C. S. Lewis, *Surprised by Joy: The Shape of My Early Life* (HarperOne, 2017).
2 Jennie Evelyn Hussey, "Lead Me to Calvary," Integrity's Hosanna! Music and Word Music (a division of Word Music), 1997.
3 Saint Isaac the Syrian, *The Ascetical Homilies of Saint Isaac the Syrian*, trans. The Holy Transfiguration Monastery (Holy Transfiguration Monastery, 2011).
4 Thomas Watson, *The Beatitudes: or A Discourse upon Part of Christs Famous Sermon on the Mount* (Ralph Smith at the Bible in Cornhill, 1660).
5 Augustus Toplady, *Free-will and Merit Fairly Examined: or, Men Not Their Own Saviors: The Substance of a Sermon Preached in the Parish Church of St. Anne, Black-Friars, London on Wednesday, May 25, 1774* (J. Matthews, 1775), 25.
6 Robert Robinson, "Come Thou Fount of Every Blessing," 1757.
7 Kathleen Norris, *Acedia and Me: A Marriage, Monks, and a Writer's Life* (Penguin Publishing Group, 2010).
8 Ludwig Koehler, *The Hebrew and Aramaic Lexicon of the Old Testament* (Brill Academic Pub, 2002).
9 Charles Dickens, *A Tale of Two Cities: A Story of the French Revolution* (Dover Publications, 1998).

10 "Justice," *ATS Bible Dictionary*, StudyLight.org, 2025, https://www.studylight.org/dictionaries/eng/ats/j/justice.html.
11 Jonathan Sacks, "Do You Think the Holocaust Represented a Failure of Humanity? (Q2.1)," The Rabbi Sacks Legacy, April 18, 2020, YouTube video, https://www.youtube.com/watch?v=6P2_9RBnLko&t=1s.
12 *Contact*, directed by Robert Zemeckis (Burbank, CA: Warner Bros. Pictures, 1997), author's paraphrase.
13 Immanuel Kant, *The Universal Natural History and Theory of the Heavens*, trans. Ian Johnston (Vancouver Island University, 2008).
14 Friedrich Nietzsche, *Thus Spake Zarathustra: A Book for All and None*, trans. Thomas Common (George Allen & Unwin, 1909), Fourth Part, "Zarathustra's Discourses," LXVII, "The Ugliest Man."
15 Friedrich Nietzsche, *The Gay Science: With a Prelude in Rhymes and an Appendix of Songs*, trans. Walter Kaufmann (Vintage, 1974), 181.
16 Corrie ten Boom, *The Hiding Place* (Chosen Books, 2006).
17 Elie Wiesel, *Night* (Hill and Wang, 2006).
18 Siddur Ashkenaz, "Shabbat, Kabbalat Shabbat, Lekha Dodi," trans. Avrohom Davis (based on the *Metsudah Linear Siddur*, 1981).
19 Gary Wiens, *Bridal Intercession: Authority in Prayer Through Intimacy with Jesus* (Oasis House, 2001).
20 Wiens, *Bridal Intercession*.
21 Bonnie Saul Wilks, *Sabbath: A Gift of Time* (Gateway Press, 2018).
22 Peter Marshall, *The Light and the Glory* (Revell, 2009).
23 *Love Story*, directed by Arthur Hiller (Hollywood: Paramount Pictures, 1970), film.

ABOUT THE AUTHOR

BONNIE SAUL WILKS moved to a kibbutz in Israel after graduating Bible school, where she served as a Christian volunteer for two and a half years. She studied Hebrew and grew to love the Jewish people and culture. Later, Bonnie and her husband and daughter were sent out from a church in Texas to pioneer Bible schools. While traveling internationally, they learned to weep with those that mourn and rejoice with the happy. For forty years Bonnie has been capturing the beauty and pain of the nations in poetry and prose and does her best writing in the Scottish highlands or the Sinai desert. She has also authored *Sabbath: A Gift of Time*, which is a glimpse of the benefits of the Jewish tradition of taking a day of rest weekly. Bonnie lives in Bedford, Texas, with her husband, where she dotes on her daughter, son-in-love, and three grandchildren.

 @roadmaptojoy    bonniewilks.com

www.ingramcontent.com/pod-product-compliance
Lightning Source LLC
Chambersburg PA
CBHW050527100526
44581CB00009B/157/J